## ONE DAY

---

**8:00 A.M.**
The phone calls stop when the children come in to see their father. . . . the President of the United States makes haste to drop his toast, his knife, pat his mouth, move the breakfast tray aside, and brace himself for the hugs, the kisses. . . .

**11:00 P.M.**
The President finishes his work. He puts the folder down on the couch, turns all the papers right side up, and sits for a moment in thought. He closes his eyes and rubs the lids with his fingers. This is the lonely time. . . .

---

THIS IS THE STORY OF A TYPICAL DAY IN THE WHITE HOUSE, AS JOHN F. KENNEDY LIVED IT. THIS IS ALSO A HISTORIC DOCUMENT WHICH SHEDS NEW LIGHT ON THE MARTYRED PRESIDENT AS A HUMAN BEING AND AS A WORLD LEADER.

Books by Jim Bishop

THE DAY LINCOLN WAS SHOT

THE DAY CHRIST DIED

# A DAY
# IN THE LIFE OF
# PRESIDENT KENNEDY

BY
JIM BISHOP

BANTAM BOOKS
TORONTO · NEW YORK · LONDON

*This low-priced Bantam Book
has been completely reset in a type face
designed for easy reading, and was printed
from new plates. It contains the complete
text of the original hard-cover edition.*
NOT ONE WORD HAS BEEN OMITTED.

A DAY IN THE LIFE OF PRESIDENT KENNEDY
*A Bantam Book / published by arrangement with
Random House, Inc.*

PRINTING HISTORY

*Random House edition published March 1964*
*2nd printing . . March 1964*
*3rd printing . . March 1964*
*4th printing . . March 1964*
*5th printing . . March 1964*

*Appeared in* GOOD HOUSEKEEPING *March 1964*

*Condensation appeared in* PHILADELPHIA BULLETIN *April 1964*
*Condensations also appeared in* CHICAGO'S AMERICAN,
CLEVELAND PRESS, CHARLOTTE *(N.C.)* OBSERVER,
MIAMI HERALD, BOSTON RECORD AMERICAN, *and*
NEW YORK JOURNAL-AMERICAN.

*Catholic Digest Book Club edition published July 1964*

*Best-in-Books (Literary Guild) edition published October 1964*

*Bantam edition published October 1964*

*Front cover photo by Cecil Stoughton.
Back cover photo by Robert Phillips*

Dedicated with Affection
to
Caroline and John F. Kennedy, Jr.
who will some day want to recall
what it was like

# FOR THE RECORD:

The phone call came in midsummer of 1963. I was at home. The man on the other end was Joseph Willicombe, Jr., an executive of King Features Syndicate. Mr. Willicombe is a man who converses as though at prayer. "Venice and I just got back from Hyannisport," he said. "We were guests of Larry Newman. Remember him? He used to work for I.N.S. Anyway, he lives next to the Kennedy compound. Somehow we got around to talking about you and how you wrote *The Day Lincoln Was Shot* and 'A Day in the Life of Eisenhower,' and so forth, and we wondered if you'd like to do a day about Kennedy."

I thought about it a moment. "Yes," I said, "I'd like to do it, Joe, and it's a great idea, but it has one weakness. Most men in high places—and especially their wives—don't like to discuss their private lives and personal habits."

"Suppose he said yes?"

I agreed that in that event I would be happy to try.

A week later Mr. Willicombe was back on the phone. "Pierre Salinger has discussed it with the President, and he says he likes the idea. Do you want to go up to Hyannisport?"

I said no. People do not think of him as a man of Hyannisport; he is the President, and that means the White House. I would prefer to see him there.

"All right," Willicombe said. "Suppose you call Salinger when you're ready, and set the date."

I did. Mr. Salinger was cordial, and I outlined with him what was necessary to produce an accurate and full story:

1. I would have to spend four days in the White House to get one representative day. The reason for this is that unexpected and unusual things might occur on several days and I wanted an average routine day. 2. The President would have to issue a directive to his assistants, his staff, the Secret Service, the White House ushers, and the personal servants to assist me with their recollections. 3. It would be necessary to see Mrs. Kennedy, and the private quarters of the family, in order to complete the portrait.

These were not arbitrary conditions imposed by a writer. They were necessary to the story, and if any one of them was impossible, the result would not be a fair representation of a day in the life of the President. Pierre Salinger understood. He consulted Mr. Kennedy, and the conditions were approved. All that remained was to set the time.

I asked Mr. Salinger if it was true that Mrs. Kennedy, who had recently sustained the loss of a newborn baby, would go to Greece for a rest. He said yes. I said that in that case I would wait until she returned. We agreed that the days October 21 to 24 would be good ones.

Kelly Bishop—my wife and assistant—spent the four days in the White House with me. The research worked out well. As I interviewed the President and the First Lady, and everyone else who had a daily bearing on their lives, Kelly made notes on decorations, attire, and attitudes.

On the twenty-fourth I had a farewell visit with Mr. Kennedy. He asked me if I had enough material for a book. I said I thought so. He said he had read my book about Lincoln. He seemed fascinated, in a melancholy way, with the accidental succession of events of that day which led to the assassination.

The President was in the best of health, and he discussed the campaign he would have to wage for a second term. He felt that it was going to be a difficult one. For what it was worth I said I was sure he would win.

I told him that I was about to leave, with Mrs. Bishop, for a vacation in Aruba, and that I would write the book there and send it on to him for possible corrections. The President seemed surprised. "Corrections?" he said. Yes, I said, corrections. I already had 168 pages of notes and I was aware of one repeated error—the wrong name of an American ambassador—and I hoped Mr. Kennedy and Mrs. Kennedy and Mr. Salinger and others would examine the manuscript carefully for similar errors. They would not have any license to change or alter an unpalatable truth, but I wanted them to feel free to spot blunders. He promised to help.

I said good-bye. He wished me well.

In Aruba, I spent almost all of my waking time writing the book. Normally I pace the writing of a book steadily—two thousand words a day. This one flowed so naturally that it was finished in twelve days. I wrote it in the present tense because I felt that the reader should feel that he is in the White House with the President and his family, watching them at their multitudinous tasks and joys.

On November 17 my wife and I were in Palm Beach having dinner at a restaurant. I saw Pierre Salinger come in. I also saw Kenneth O'Donnell, the President's appointments secretary. They joined us. President Kennedy was in Florida, it seemed, to make a few political speeches. He would return to Washington and then make another political appearance, this time in Texas. I got the impression that Mr. Kennedy was prepared to lose most of the South in the 1964 campaign, but would fight hard for the electoral votes of Florida and Texas, where he felt he had a chance.

We talked chaff. The President had been offshore that morning to watch a Polaris missile fired from a submarine under the surface. "Your name came up," Mr. Salinger said, "and the President asked if you had finished the manuscript. He seems anxious to see it." That was strange. I wondered why the President would think of such a relatively insignificant thing when his days were filled with such enormous problems. I finally decided that, as a man who had never permitted—or assisted in—a personal portrait of his private and public life, he may have been concerned about whether it would turn out to be a critical book.

"I'm leaving for Japan on Tuesday," Mr. Salinger said. This was Sunday night. "If you can get me a copy of the manuscript, I'll read it on the plane and have my suggestions ready for the President when I get back." I promised to see what I could do. Back home in New Jersey, my secretary, Mrs. Ralph Walter, and her husband agreed to drive to Washington on Monday, November 18, and deliver the manuscript to the White House.

On Tuesday, Mr. Salinger, Dean Rusk, and others left for Japan. On Friday, November 22, Mr. Salinger was reading the manuscript in Honolulu while Mr. and Mrs. Kennedy were acknowledging the applause of great crowds in Dallas.

Slowly, the President's smiling face moved into the cross-hairs of a rifle. In a moment, the world paused to gasp. In a moment, a gallant lady was holding the bleeding head of her husband on the lap of her pink wool suit. In a moment, there was no President.

To my eternal sorrow, I was the last writer to work with President Kennedy on an exclusive story. Therefore I asked to have it published as it was written, without anything added or changed, when the world was bright for him and the future held the warm promise of goodness and victory. What you will read in this book is a portrait of the Kennedy family as it looked then—with no premonition that, for him, time had run out.

*Jim Bishop*

NOVEMBER 29, 1963

# A DAY IN THE LIFE OF PRESIDENT KENNEDY

# 7:00 A.M.

---

The sun, like almost everyone in Washington, is on time. It comes up from a hummock of tall pin oaks and poplars on Capitol Heights, throws a pink spangle at the statue of Freedom atop the Capitol, and paints the granite shaft of the Washington Monument from the top down. The streets are in blue shadow. The flowers in the little formal gardens of Georgetown hang their heads heavily and plots of grass have aged overnight with the silver of hoarfrost.

The cardinals and bluejays are awake first, and they curve and bank the shuttle service between trees, always eager to assert their rights over the majority—the sparrows. The early buses snort and sigh from corner to corner; sugar-cube milk trucks complete their rounds and tinkle with the music of empty bottles; the statue of a general in Lafayette Park throws a longer shadow than he did in life; the mist in the Tidal Basin lies lightly on the bosom of the water; on the White House lawn a gray squirrel sits transfixed, aching to be friendly but forever afraid.

It is a good morning, a morning of cool loveliness and exalted promise; a morning on which the breeze from the south is so slight, so lazy, that it spins the leaves of the poplars in slow motion, like a magician turning his hands to show that he has nothing up his sleeve; a morning when a far-off plane appears to be pinned to the cobalt-blue; a morning when parents sit at breakfast with their children, smiling behind their authoritative masks at the chatter of their own magpies.

This good feeling pervades the being of George Edward Thomas, who steps out of Room 324 in the east hall of the White House and closes the door softly behind him. He pats his black bow tie once more, then hefts the newspapers under his arm. George Thomas is fifty-five. He comes down the hall with the stumpy walk of a man who has spent a lot of time on his feet. He is a cherubic-looking Negro, with roundnesses in successive sizes, starting with the eyes and working toward the face and then the figure. He has been the President's valet since 1947, when John F. Kennedy was a freshman member of the House of Representatives.

Mr. Thomas pauses at the private elevator, looks up at the indicator, and decides not to wait for it. He walks down the curving marble steps to the second floor, through the dining-room door,

4

and into the kitchen. Nick, a cook, looks up. He too has a good-morning smile. Nick is a Filipino who learned to cook when he was in the United States Navy. He and George Thomas have coffee and exchange the small talk of men who walk the same beat. Nick always marvels that George never needs an alarm clock. The valet can go to sleep at one A.M. or two, and still awaken at precisely six-thirty. But now that George is awake, he keeps looking at the clock. He talks awhile longer, sipping coffee and watching the big hand sneak imperceptibly toward six.

In the east wing of the White House, Floyd Boring looks up and sees that the time is almost seven-thirty. Normally he takes the eight-to-four shift of the Secret Service. Last night he assumed the late shift. In the west wing, a police sergeant sits back in a swivel chair, in the soft somnolence of a man who is awake, but not truly. On the second floor, Maud Shaw, the children's nurse, supervises the washing and dressing of the gleefully shouting Miss Caroline Kennedy, six, and Master John F. Kennedy, Jr., three.

On the ground floor of this long, bar-bell-shaped building, the first shaft of sunlight pierces the security of the President's office. It has slanted across the south lawn, passed the old rose garden, and entered the oval-shaped room through the tall French doors.

The high-backed black leather chair is imposing. The big mahogany desk, with the Great Seal of the United States on its face, was given to President McKinley by Queen Victoria. The oval rug matches the contours of the room. It is pale green but looks deeper in color now because the sun has not yet reached it. The top of the desk is neat—a blotter, a desk set, a photograph frame which holds a list of the President's appointments for yesterday, and some ivory mementos; opposite the desk there is a fireplace, flanked by two beige-covered sofas, a rocking chair presented by the crew of the carrier *Kitty Hawk,* and some wall paintings of naval battles of the War of 1812.

At seven-thirty two Secret Service men enter the office. They are about to undertake a task which is done frequently, but not every day. One crouches along the perimeter of the wall and moves slowly around the office. In his hand is a Geiger counter. He will test every object in the room for radioactivity. Later, and unobtrusively, he will pass the counter over the President's wristwatch.

The man does not expect to find anything alarming. Nor does his confrere, who unscrews the transmitter of both presidential telephones. He is looking for a transistor radio—the size of a girl's fingernail—which can be hidden in a telephone. Both phones have attached "scramblers" which render all presidential conversation unintelligible except at the recipient's end of the

6

line—but a tiny transistor could pick the words up before they are scrambled and broadcast them a short distance, where they could be relayed to anyone who is interested.

American intelligence of all branches—C.I.A., F.B.I., and U. S. Army—are aware that the newest method of subtle assassination is to plant a minuscule amount of radioactive material on the person of the victim, or close to him. Abroad, some political figures who have died of so-called natural causes have been found to have their rings and watches pierced with tiny holes. Inside was uranium; in all cases the death was slow and nauseous, similar to pernicious anemia or leukemia.

On the second floor, George Thomas taps his mouth with a napkin, looks at the wall clock once more, and says: "About twenty or twenty-five minutes, Nick," meaning the President will be ready for breakfast then. George leaves the little kitchen and walks into the private quarters of the Kennedy family in the west wing of the mansion. He has the newspapers—*The New York Times*, the *Washington Post*, the *St. Louis Post-Dispatch*, the *Wall Street Journal*—and he strides through the sitting room, across the soft rugs, and into a door on the left. Mr. Thomas places the newspapers on the bed of the small bedroom, which is empty. He walks softly into a bathroom, and taps lightly on another bedroom door at the far side.

"Mr. President," he whispers hoarsely. "It's close to seven-thirty."

The time is closer to seven-forty. Mr. Thomas listens, and hears a clearing of the throat. The President of the United States is awake. Unlike some of his predecessors, he requires no time for collecting his wits, yawning, or a second rap on the door. He is out of bed at once, quickly and quietly. The metamorphosis from deep slumber to keen alertness is about ten seconds.

He walks through a foyer to the empty bedroom. "Good morning, George," the President says. George is busy pulling the drapes back and closing the windows. "Morning, Mr. President," he says. Mr. Kennedy props the pillows on the bed. He puts a robe on over his nightshirt (George calls it a topcoat) and lies on the bed with his newspapers. Few persons can read with the speed and absorption of this man. As his hazel eyes traverse staggering mountains of eight-point type, it seems as though he is reading vertically, rather than from left to right. Within fifteen minutes he can read four newspapers and be prepared to discuss every story of consequence in any of them.

He devours thoughts, ideas, and reports. The President reads a story with care, even though it is based on a statement made by him—or rather, more especially if it originated with him. Newspapers have been the sounding board of presidents for over a hundred years, but no other president has listened so hard to find out if what he has said induces the echo of warm applause or cold mockery.

Most presidents assume office with hopeful solicitude toward the press. In time, the criticisms of the newspapers, even those who espouse a president's cause, raise welts on the sensibilities of the chief of state; and like Harry Truman and Dwight D. Eisenhower, Mr. Kennedy tended to skip reading the columns and editorials of those he felt had betrayed him. Once he announced that the *New York Herald-Tribune* would no longer be delivered at the White House, but this helped neither himself nor his program, and so the paper was reinstated.

John F. Kennedy is no happier with the press than his predecessors, but he now reads his critics as assiduously as those who attest his greatness.

George Thomas has finished drawing the President's bath. He goes to the wardrobe closet and begins to lay out the attire for today. It consists of a blue suit, a white shirt, black shoes, a plain dark tie and socks. It is wrong, in the case of President Kennedy, to refer to any suit of clothes as the "attire for today," because the President redresses from the skin out at least twice a day, even on a day such as this one when no public functions are scheduled. He averages three, and sometimes four, shirts each day. (The President has between fifteen and eighteen suits of clothes and about eight pairs of shoes.)

The President prefers a tub to a shower. He bathes as he does everything else: purposefully and forthrightly. He treats time as though he has been told he has a week to live. From the first waking moment until the last, the President moves at flank speed. He comes out of the bathroom, bathed and shaved and brushed, in a terry-cloth robe, and he moves toward his breakfast tray as though this too is a task to be accomplished in stride.

# 8:00 A.M.

Mr. Kennedy's associates refer to him as a meat-and-potatoes man. This implies that his taste for food is simple. It is. He finds little time for savoring food, or for educating his palate to the subtleties of flavor. His breakfast, for example, is almost always the same: large glass of orange juice, toast and jelly, two four-and-a-half-minute eggs, broiled bacon, and coffee with cream and sugar.

The President sits in a wing chair, eating and making phone calls. Usually the calls are to presidential assistants, and they are largely inspired by what he has read in the morning newspapers. He phones Kenneth O'Donnell, his appointments secretary—and it is a minor source of irritation to O'Donnell, as it is to all other assistants, that the President sees stories which have escaped their notice.

"Ken," he says, "have you seen the corn-surplus story on page fourteen of the *Times?* No? Well, read it and ask Freeman to stop in to see me around ten." Or he may call Theodore Sorensen, foreign affairs advisor, speech writer, member of the National Security Council. "Ted, have you read the Gromyko speech in Leningrad? Well, it's on page four of the *Washington Post* and I wish you would check it out with Rusk [Secretary of State] and Kohler [U. S. Ambassador to the Soviet Union] and find out if it represents a change of view on Cuba."

Only rarely does he receive calls. No one disturbs the President at breakfast unless the matter is too important to wait until he arrives at the office. Since the close of World War II, the most powerful political adversary of the United States —and the potential military one—has remained the Union of Socialist Soviet Republics, and the time zone in Moscow is eight hours ahead of the time in Washington. In a conflict of chronic tensions, Russia has the advantage, because whatever Moscow wants to say in the matter of explosive utterances can be said at ten A.M. Moscow time, which is two A.M. Washington time. Whatever the matter may be, it is often difficult to decide whether the President should be awakened to deal with it at once.

The phone calls stop when the children come in to see their father. At a few minutes past eight they run pellmell through the second-floor hall from their rooms to his. It is impossible to assess which side draws more joy from these wild and noisy sessions, but it is a certainty that Caroline,

John-John, and Mrs. Kennedy are the only people who cause the President to forget the clock.

They arrive at top speed, banking the turns in
their robes and slippers, and the President of the
United States makes haste to drop his toast, his
knife, pat his mouth, move the breakfast tray
aside, and brace himself for the hugs, the kisses,
the high excitement of childish conversation, a
cascade of words which tumble and intermingle
so that only they know what they are talking
about.

Caroline has more reserve than little John. She
shows her father a paper on which she has
printed her first name twenty times in large block
letters. The President studies it and leans back,
obviously overcome and a little awed at the ac-
complishment. "Caroline!" he says, spending each
word separately. "Did . . . you . . . do . . . this?"
She nods her head, almost shy with pride, and
this calls for a congratulatory kiss.

Both children have almost honey-blond hair.
Both are active and energetic types, like their
parents. Little John swoops around the bedroom
carrying a red-plush box. "Look at my due-ry
box," he says. His father looks at it. It is empty,
but he is impelled to react as though it were the
wonder of the age. The President does not want
his son to be called "Jack" or "Johnny." To em-
phasize the point, he addresses the boy as John-
John.

"Next Saturday," he says, pointing a finger over the top of Caroline, "we're going to ride the helicopter again." John-John drops the jewelry box and jumps with glee. He loves aircraft. "We're going to Camp David," the President says to Caroline, "and you can ride the horses."

They talk about Caroline's schoolwork, about an imaginary character called Floppy-Ears, and about their five dogs. These range in size from a big lean Irish wolfhound named Wolf, to a German shepherd called Clipper whose monotonous ambition is to chase a thrown piece of wood, down to a slightly ruffled cocker spaniel, Shannon, who asserts himself against the larger dogs. They sleep in a room on the south side of the ground floor, between the flower room and the swimming pool.

Mr. Kennedy is conscious of the importance of full-time parenthood; so conscious, in fact, that he often interrupts meetings of state to be with the children. Only recently he began to arrange his evening swim so that Caroline and John-John could join him, and now this event is established practice. When Mrs. Kennedy is away, he arranges his schedule so that he can spend extra time with the children.

For a time both parents worried about the effect on the youngsters of life in the White House, which is a hurly-burly of splendor, sycophancy, and security. But Mrs. Kennedy has succeeded in keeping a private, normal family life, with time for conversation, time for reading, time for personal friends, time for private recreation in a park, on a farm, on the water. Perhaps because of her efforts, the worries of the Kennedys about the effect of public adulation on the children proved groundless. Both children understand that their father is President of the United States, but they do not appreciate what it means. If there is a difference between their lives and the lives of other children, it is that no matter where they go, one or two Secret Service men walk behind them. However, as neither child understands the meaning of Secret Service, they think of these men as helpful friends of Daddy and Mummy.

Miss Shaw, the children's nurse, stands outside the President's bedroom and calls the children. They run out as swiftly as they arrived. The President finishes his breakfast, and begins to dress. Sometimes George Thomas hands the clothes to Mr. Kennedy. At other times—if the President's back is paining him—he assists with donning socks and shoes and trousers.

The presidential back has received much attention in the world press, but it is not a serious medical matter. Below the lumbar region, in the sacroiliac area, tendons and nerve areas are chronically irritated. Heat treatment, massage, and infrared radiation do little more than ameliorate pain. The President masks this pain well, and is reconciled to the fact that it is something which will come and go and might be with him for the rest of his life.

This morning he dresses by himself. Then he picks up a folder of "homework"—mostly problems of state, speeches, and written briefings and recommendations which he has digested and annotated between dinnertime last night and bedtime —and steps out of the bedroom into the sitting room. If Mrs. Kennedy is up, he spends some time with her. Usually they discuss the predictable events of the day. If she is still sleeping, he cautions the children against making undue noise and sits on a couch near the big west window, his legs crossed, and studies the folder of work once more.

In the west wing a dark slender woman walks through the maze of offices and corridors toward the President's office. She is Mrs. Evelyn Lincoln, private secretary to the President. She wears glasses and looks vaguely like a brunette Bette Davis. She has a slight, shy sense of humor which dies when some politician says heartily: "Well, it's good to have a Lincoln back in the White House."

Mrs. Lincoln arrives a few minutes after eight, and goes directly to her bright pleasant office. Most of the time she keeps the door between her office and the President's ajar, so that if he calls her she can hear him. She has worked for Mr. Kennedy for over ten years, and with his phenomenal rise to power, her work has increased. The presidential mail is an example. It amounts, on the average, to 30,000 pieces each week, or about 5,000 each mail-delivery day.

It is sorted in the offices of the old State Department Building, across the street from the White House. Out of the pile about a hundred letters reach the desk of Mrs. Lincoln each morning. These are considered important enough to warrant her attention. Of the remainder, every fiftieth unsolicited letter is taken from the pile at random and placed in a folder. The President reads these to get a good cross section of public opinion.

The total of private and random mail is two hundred letters. Mrs. Lincoln gives these her personal screening when she arrives, and can usually cut the total in half by redirecting inquiries to the proper government departments. All phone calls to the President go through her desk. She is subject to the unremitting pressures of all—from the Vice-President down to the newest stenographer in the press secretary's office. Mrs. Lincoln is one of three direct avenues to Mr. Kennedy. The others are Kenneth O'Donnell, his appointments secretary, and Pierre Salinger, his press secretary. However, most of the four hundred employees within the White House, who "must" see the President "at once," ask Mrs. Lincoln to intercede for them. Anyone from the pantry boy on up, who, for example, wants an autographed photo of the President, will usually consult Mrs. Lincoln. Thus, as Mr. Kennedy sits at his desk he faces three doors—the one at the left belongs to O'Donnell; the one at the center is used occasionally by Salinger; the one at the right, slightly ajar, is Mrs. Lincoln's.

The President places the folder under his arm, and leaves his quarters. At the elevator two Secret Service men are waiting. They fall into step with him after an exchange of morning greetings. They ride to the ground floor, and as they step off, they turn left into a corridor, then right to get to the west wing. They pass a White House policeman, on station in the red-carpeted hall, who salutes. The President nods, smiles briefly, and steps briskly toward the greenhouse and the colonnades which lead past the rose garden to his office.

It is eight-twenty and the White House has been coming alive with cumulative speed. Kenneth O'Donnell is already in his office, and the presidential appointment list for the day has been typed and inserted in the picture frame on Mr. Kennedy's desk; copies have been passed around to other offices. O'Donnell's assistants and secretaries are at work on the day's plans.

A round-faced young lady arrives on the Pennsylvania Avenue side of the White House and is escorted up to the third floor. She is Alice Grimes, who teaches the private first-grade elementary school in the White House. On the top floor she walks past George Thomas's room and then turns right and walks up an incline behind the coping of the roof. On top is a medium-sized squarish room with a good view of the lawn, stretching a third of a mile to the south. There is a small pond and a huge effervescent fountain within her view as she removes her hat and makes her classroom ready.

At the west gate, newspaper reporters and television photographers begin to move in. Each is challenged or accorded a good morning by the White House policemen in sentry boxes; each carries White House Correspondent credentials. A man with an elegant smile comes through the gate. He is J. Bernard West, chief usher of the White House. He is, in effect, master of the household. Very little ever happens within the main part of the mansion which has not survived his scrutiny and approbation.

Two minutes behind him is a good-looking woman with mahogany skin. She wears an amiable regality and a barely repressed sense of humor on a handsome face. She is Mrs. Providencia Paredes, personal maid to Mrs. Kennedy. She was born in San Pedro Macoris, Santo Domingo, thirty-seven years ago. Mrs. Paredes supports her mother and two growing sons. She goes to the third floor, where she has a room near the private school. There she picks up a phone and asks the White House operators if they have awakened Mrs. Kennedy yet. She is told yes. Mrs. Paredes hangs up, then walks down to the private quarters on the second floor.

A minute ahead of her, McGeorge Bundy, the President's assistant in charge of foreign affairs, arrives in the west wing. He is youngish, broad-faced, wears glasses, and is balding. He has already concluded a half hour of volley tennis, and he walks quickly down to the back offices he uses —with his staff—for national security. Major General C. V. Clifton, tall, ramrod-straight even when at his ease, waits for him. Clifton is the President's military aide, and he works closely with Bundy and the Department of Defense.

One hundred and fifty yards away on the east side of the White House, the eight-to-four shift of the Secret Service arrives and is checked out for duty. Down the hall from their office, Nancy Tuckerman, social secretary to the First Lady, arrives at her desk. She is young and gracious and alert, and to her falls the responsibility of carrying out the explicit directions of Mrs. Kennedy in matters ranging all the way from who sits where at a state dinner, to why the lighting is dim in the East Room.

Miss Tuckerman has two stenographers to assist with correspondence, which is of such magnitude that Mrs. Kennedy too gets a folder of "homework" to pore over in the late hours. Pamela Turnure, a brunette pixyish girl, arrives. She is Mrs. Kennedy's press secretary, possibly the first of her kind.

In the press office, Christine Camp is now at her desk. She assists Pierre Salinger. Helen Ganss, who has worked in the press department since President Truman's time, adjusts her snowy hair to its fluffiest, and shares some coffee with the newest worker, a stenographer with a Miss America figure, Nancy Larson. David Powers walks into O'Donnell's office. He is a bald second-generation Irishman from Boston, the President's crony. Powers has the wonderment of a priest in his eyes, and the tickle of blarney on his tongue. He is not only the best raconteur in the White House, but he has the sharpest memory for detail.

The main White House kitchen is filling with chefs, cooks, waiters, and dishwashers. Captain Seckel of the White House police sits like a Latin Buddha behind his desk in the press reception room. Samuel Mitchell, the Negro major-domo of the reception room, stands behind his desk with fingertips barely touching the wood, watching through his glasses as two assistants jump to their morning work of distributing newspapers and messages, and escorting visitors to the proper offices.

On the south lawn, four men push blowing machines across the grass. They pile the fallen leaves into isolated mounds, to be swept up and carried away later in the day. It is eight forty-five and the official day is beginning. A policeman at the southwest gate checks a small truck bringing delicacies for the official table. The vehicle, the driver, and all packages are examined, unless the policeman knows the truck as a "regular."

Mrs. Paredes, called "Provey" by everyone, opens the drapes in Mrs. Kennedy's room and pulls back the curtains facing south and west. The First Lady is not only stunningly handsome; she has the distressing habit of looking cheerful and attractive even when she first awakens. Provey has been Jacqueline Kennedy's maid for ten years, and cannot remember one morning in which her presence did not evoke a big smile, a lazy good morning, and the solicitous conversation of two women who understand each other. Mrs. Paredes has a slight Spanish accent, and her brand of English is sometimes an improvement over the correct word. The President considers Provey one of the most intelligent persons in the White House.

Mrs. Kennedy slips into a dressing robe and has breakfast in bed. The breakfast is appetizing: scrambled eggs, two strips of bacon, toast, orange juice, honey, a glass of skim milk—sometimes tea, sometimes coffee. Provey makes no comment on what Mrs. Kennedy does with breakfast, but she feels that her mistress does not eat enough. The bath is drawn while the food is aggravated from one side of the plate to the other, and little of it is consumed. This hurts Provey, who, at home, often says to her mother: "How she keep alive dat way?" John often has breakfast with his mother and usually eats all her honey and bacon.

Sometimes Mrs. Kennedy wears tortoise-shell glasses at night to read. In the morning she reads without them. Her personal secretary, Mary Gallagher, is outside in the sitting room waiting for the morning dictation to begin. When the bath is ready, Mrs. Kennedy is ready. Like the President, she plans ahead, parcels her time carefully, and somehow manages to be wife, mother, household manager, and First Lady. Provey lays out casual clothes for the morning—beige slacks, beige orlon sweater, and dark-brown flat shoes, gleaming. No adornments, no jewelry.

Miss Shaw permits Caroline to run in and kiss her mother good-bye before attending school. John-John dashes in and wants to know, "Where we going to go?" He always wants to know, and it doesn't matter how often he gets a reply, he wants to know anew. Mrs. Kennedy has a wonderful way with children. She has more than love; she has understanding. In the bedlam around her, she can continue a conversation with Provey, not hearing and yet sensitive to the play screams of her children; but if there is a scream of another pitch, she is alert to it by reflex and is on her feet hurrying toward the sound before she knows the cause. If there is a crash, she jumps too, but when she finds that it is not a child who fell, just an expensive painting knocked down, she smiles with relief. She is attuned to children; not merely her own, but all children.

She talks to Caroline with an arm around the child, smiling archly at the little girlish triumphs, frowning and almost mirroring her daughter's expression if matters are not going right. There is a farewell kiss, and Miss Shaw escorts Caroline to the third floor to class.

In the main lobby of the White House, her classmates start to arrive. There are seven little girls, four boys. They are not the progeny of government people *per se;* in the main, they are the sons and daughters of old friends of the Kennedys from their Georgetown days. The idea of a small school started in 1962, when Mrs. Kennedy and her friends brought the children to a different house one day each week, and had Elizabeth Boyd, a kindergarten teacher, organize them into a play group.

The Kennedys do not pay for the little private school on the third floor. The cost of teacher, desks, and small open lockers is shared by the parents of all students. The ten children who do not live in the White House arrive each morning in a car-pool arrangement. They stand in the main lobby until the last one arrives; then they are taken upstairs. Each brings his lunchbox.

At eight forty-five the class is called to order. The sun is now fairly high, and it slants in off the back of the room. Hair is tidy, little frocks and suits are neat, and hands are clasped on the edge of desks. Sweaters are hung on pegs in the plywood lockers. Miss Grimes begins by discussing what day this is, and what date.

She seldom sits, preferring to walk around the small class as she talks. Sometimes she sits in the back of the room, still talking, or asking questions. If there is a presidential reception on the south lawn for a visiting chief of state, with its twenty-one-gun salute of cannon, the barking orders to the military, the strains of national anthems coming from the red-coated U. S. Marine Band, the teacher will recess class for a few moments so that the children can press their noses to the windows and see the excitement.

At other, duller, times, Miss Grimes discusses the projects of the first grade for the day. Then she will begin to read a story, and ask each child in turn to pick up the thread of it and read on a little further. She is patient with her charges, but firm in the discipline of learning. She insists that, on arrival, each child shake hands with her and say: "Good morning, Miss Grimes." She also makes certain that each student studies French at least four days each week. During this period the teacher does not permit the children to speak in English.

On the first floor, the President runs through his mail. Sometimes, when he is ready to dictate replies, he will not call Mrs. Lincoln to him. He will go to her desk, and stand there, calling upon his extensive vocabulary quickly and easily, making his answers succinct. Sometimes he will say: "I just heard that Joe ———— is in the hospital. Take a letter to him." On other occasions he uses an electric dictating machine, but he does not do so well in marshaling his thoughts as when he is facing Mrs. Lincoln.

Doubt is a rare condition for Mr. Kennedy's mind. Almost always he knows what he wants to say, or do, and he makes it plain that he wants to say or do it at once. His assistants rate him as a good assessor of situations. Sometimes, to their surprise, he can see something bad in good news. In an action by the Soviet Union, he sees not only what is being done, but relates it to past performance, the policy of countries friendly to Russia, and the propaganda effect on world opinion. He encourages disagreement among his close assistants; in fact, anyone in the small group around him is expected to disagree, and disagree loudly, if he feels so disposed. However, after all the discussion it is John F. Kennedy who will make the decision, and once he makes it, all hands abide by it whether they find it palatable or not.

Pierre Salinger is in his office. He leans back, puffs on a long cigar, and places his heels on the desk. He is dark and sturdy, almost chubby, and gives the appearance of total relaxation, but his reflexes betray tension. For a heavy man, he can come to his feet faster than most men can sit.

In Mrs. Lincoln's office, the President concludes the immediate mail. Other letters are on his desk, but the urgent ones are taken care of. Mrs. Lincoln gives the President a sheaf of mail sent to Cabinet officers and ranking members of his official family—mail which they hesitate to answer without presidential direction. This adds to his daily workload, but he takes it back into his office with him.

On a small table near Mrs. Lincoln's desk, there are square chunks of milk chocolate on a plate. They are there to tempt any visitor, but Mr. Kennedy has never eaten one. He does not eat candy at any time, and he is averse to between-meal snacks. As he turns to leave, he says softly: "Tell Ken I want to see him."

# 9:00 A.M.

All over the White House the soft sporadic chatter is heard. The secretaries study their notes, frowning, then stare at the sheet of letterhead paper in their machines, and the letters form into words, the words become sentences which trail across the paper in neat, evenly spaced thoughts. The dials on file cabinets are spun, and the drawers are opened. Pencils break, and are resharpened. Little red lights glow on telephones, and the receivers are lifted. Messengers arrive, leave something, and depart. Men read mail, and talk into gray electric machines.

Intelligence comes into the White House, and intelligence leaves the White House. It ranges from the most important top-secret memorandum from the President to Secretary of Defense Robert McNamara, down to one which states: "Deliver about 12:30—one cont. milk; one tomato and lettuce on white toast—please skip the mayonnaise." The White House telephone operators swing the trunk jacks into position, and take calls from near and from far; the direct-wire lines to many parts of official Washington are in use. On the second floor, Mrs. Kennedy is dressed and ready for the busy schedule of the average day.

In the east wing, Nancy Tuckerman studies a cardboard replica of a huge U-shaped table in the State Dining Room, and sticks colored bits of paper with names on them in the correct places. This will be a state luncheon for a Latin-American chief of state tomorrow, and the seating arrangements are always more important than the menu. The young lady's work is a matter of tiptoe diplomacy; if it is impossible to please all, then the goal must be not to offend anyone.

The office is feminine—a voodoo doll on a desk; a painting of Mrs. Kennedy on a wall; a coffee table sporting an orchid; books called *Larousse Gastronomique, Menus for Entertaining,* and *Betty Crocker's Cook Book;* a plastic basket with two dozen pens arranged like flowers; *Town and Country, Harper's, National Geographic;* files which read: "State Entertainment," "Christmas Party," "Ballet," "Garden Club," "Christmas Ballet for Children."

Miss Tuckerman phones the chief usher. The President would like to have music at tomorrow's luncheon; will Mr. West please phone the Marine Band? The remainder of the arrangements have been made some time ago: consommé, a green salad, tournedos of beef with wild rice, potatoes

Long Branch, rolls, coffee, ice cream. The time has been set to the minute. Even the pre-prandial cocktail has been arranged for the Rose Room.

If it is true—and it is—that no President worked as hard at his job as this one, then it is equally true that no First Lady ever accomplished as much in as little time as Mrs. Kennedy. She is as penurious with time as the President, but she manages to give the illusion of having all the time in the world. At nine-ten A.M. she sits in slacks, ankles crossed on the rug before her chair, dictating letters to Miss Gallagher. She appreciates the gracious phrase, the hospitable attitude. She did not court this position as First Lady, and she looked forward to it with anxiety bordering on regret. But once she became immersed in the chores of the White House, she decided to do all, be all, participate in everything, and still save enough of herself to have a family life.

Mrs. Kennedy's mail averages 2,500 to 5,000 letters per week, a fact which would have appalled Grace Goodhue Coolidge, but which would have exhilarated Mrs. Franklin D. Roosevelt. All letters are read and sorted. The personal ones are answered by Mrs. Kennedy; the others, by her secretaries. When the morning mail is completed, the First Lady confers with Pamela Turnure.

They discuss the daily program of Mrs. Kennedy, and the daily social functions scheduled. Miss Turnure writes the press releases, and they

are approved and mimeographed for the newspaper and television reporters. The burden of activity—or participation—in the affairs of the
White House which Mrs. Kennedy has imposed
upon herself can hardly be better demonstrated
than by ticking off her secretaries: one for press,
one social, one personal.

In his office, President Kennedy leans back in
his high-backed chair and regards O'Donnell.
(Against the back of the concave chair, there is
an oblong of foam rubber, as additional support
for his back.) Mr. O'Donnell, lean, hard, a Boston Irishman and father of five, looks vaguely like
James Forrestal. "It's going to be an easy day, Mr.
President," the appointments secretary says. Mr.
Kennedy glances at the calendar. He smiles. "It's
about time."

It is the softest of days. There is Secretary of
Agriculture Orval Freeman at ten; Angier Biddle
Duke of the State Department on a matter of
protocol and the President's wishes regarding a
Latin-American chief of state tomorrow, at ten-
twenty; Ted Sorensen in a few minutes—for a
few minutes; Pierre Salinger at ten forty-five for a
briefing before his press conference at eleven; the
signing of a health bill in the Cabinet Room at
eleven-thirty; Secretary of the Treasury Douglas
Dillon at twelve—for a minute or two; McGeorge
Bundy and General Clifton at three forty-five; an
ambassador with credentials at four-twenty.

That is all. There will be additional off-the-record interviews, but these are with members of the President's staff of assistants and are not part of his official calendar. He may see Powers, Salinger, Sorensen, O'Donnell, and Bundy several times during the day, depending upon his needs, and theirs. There will be phone calls, sporadically, from the Hill (the Congress), and these will be from the President's liaison men, or from his party's congressional leaders—Vice-President Lyndon Johnson, Senator Hubert Humphrey, Speaker John McCormack, and others. They will give him the latest news regarding pending legislation, the actions of congressional committees, the roll calls, the latest switches in voting strength on matters of tax bills, health measures, social legislation, defense, foreign aid, and budget. They will discuss high strategy and lost causes, cloak-room bargaining and vacillating votes, the political position of a full-time adversary and a part-time one: the Republican Party and Southern Democrats.

As a day, it must be called less than routine. A fairly average day during President Kennedy's first year in office looked something like this:

| | |
|---|---|
| 9:17-9:20 | Mr. O'Donnell |
| 9:20-9:30 | Mr. Dungan, General Goodpastor, General Clifton |
| 9:30-10:15 | Representatives of Americans for Democratic Action |

| | |
|---|---|
| 10:15-10:25 | Mr. O'Donnell |
| 10:25-10:37 | Senator Long, Congressman Willis and Mrs. Willis (Senator Long's daughter Kay, Queen of Mardi Gras Ball, and group of girls—picture) |
| 10:37-10:51 | Congressman William L. Dawson, Illinois, Chairman House Government Operations Committee (off record) |
| 10:51-11:45 | Mr. Reardon (overlapping appointment) |
| 11:30-11:45 | Secretary Dean Rusk |
| 11:50-12:06 | Dr. Glenn Seaborg, Dr. Wiesner, Mr. Bundy (off record) |
| 12:14-12:20 | Mr. Feldman |
| 12:20-12:35 | Very Reverend Francis B. Sayre, Dean of Washington National Cathedral |
| 12:35-12:50 | Secretary Douglas Dillon |
| 12:50-12:55 | Mr. O'Donnell |
| 12:55- | To White House pool and exercise |
| 1:15-2:20 | Lunch with Vice-President and Mr. and Mrs. Arthur Sulzberger, also Dr. Howard Rusk |
| 2:24- | Returned to office with Mr. and Mrs. Sulzberger and Dr. Rusk |
| 2:28-2:43 | Vice-President presents Heart Association Award to Mr. Sulzberger |
| 2:43-3:08 | Senator John L. McClellan, Arkansas (off record) |
| 3:10-3:25 | Mr. Allen Dulles |
| 3:25-3:30 | Mr. Dungan |
| 3:30-3:36 | Mr. O'Donnell |
| 3:42- | To south grounds to see Mrs. Kennedy off for country |
| 3:50- | To mansion |
| 4:00- | Back to office |

| | |
|---|---|
| 4:05-4:45 | President meets with his Science Advisory Committee in Cabinet Room |
| 4:45-5:04 | Foy Kohler, Assistant Secretary for European Affairs (off record) |
| 5:04-5:50 | Ambassador Herve Alphand, France (off record) |
| 5:50-6:20 | Mr. Sorensen |
| 6:20-6:45 | Mr. Rostow |
| 7:45- | President left office |

A day like this—in addition to the regular mail, phone calls, and so forth—calls upon a single human mind to dissociate itself from each event as it passes and concentrate completely upon the next one, or the strain would become unbearable. One of the best presidents at handling such a calendar was Eisenhower, who had the faculty of turning a mental switch off as a caller left, and turning another one on receptive to the next visitor. (Author's note: Dwight Eisenhower once told me that he could also judge how urgent the caller's business was by the way he sat.)

At nine thirty-five Mrs. Kennedy gets in a car on the south grounds with a Secret Service man and little John. She is taking him to a play school in Georgetown. As he gets into the car, he insists first that he wants to see the dogs, to ask them how they are feeling. When that fails, he says he would like to see his daddy. Failing both, he decides that it will be nice to go to play school by helicopter. He goes by car.

34

Mr. Sorensen's secretary stands in the doorway to his office. "The President is ready," she says. He nods, and gathers some material to take with him. In a sense, Theodore C. Sorensen is the top political assistant to the President, a member of the inner team, a speech writer and phrase minter, and yet he wears the mantle of a man who prefers to be alone.

Glasses and a crew cut set off a youngish intense face. He thinks with his hands clasped before him, and he thinks well enough to play a part in most presidential political decisions. He is a man of contrasts—one who can sound intellectually remote in one breath, and in the next, finger a voodoo doll on his desk or pluck a book called 10,000 *Jokes, Toasts & Stories* from a rack. He works in his shirt sleeves. Like other members of the "team"—with the exception of Salinger—Sorenson keeps a photograph of the President and a set of Sandburg's *The War Years* close at hand.

The President and Sorensen disagree often, but they are as one on the fundamentals of good government. The State Department sometimes examines a Sorensen speech to be delivered by the President, and the Rusk group feels that the young presidential assistant is often "daring." But Sorensen and the President feel that two terms— eight years—is a short time for attaining national goals. Almost every president has reached this conclusion between the first and second year of his first term. Most of them assume office feeling that all one needs is to be elected, work up a progressive program for the good of all, be of noble heart and good cheer, and wait for Congress to act.

It is in this spirit of time's-awasting that Mr. Kennedy and Sorensen devise hard-hitting "shake 'em up" speeches. Sorensen can tailor-make the speech depending upon the group to whom the President will address it. Notions on public welfare and strikes are kept on file until Mr. Kennedy is about to make an address to a labor or management group. Liberal and specific ideas about education are held until the President accepts an honorary degree from a college; material relating to space exploration is held back for a science forum address; matters relating to defense may await the launching of an aircraft carrier or a Polaris submarine. The opportunity to mend political fences and point the indicting finger at the adversaries awaits hundred-dollar testimonial dinners, or state campaigns.

Sorensen walks between filing cabinets down a checkered-linoleum hall to O'Donnell's office. He nods to the appointments secretary and to David Powers. O'Donnell nods toward the inner door, and Sorensen goes through it and into the presence of the President. They exchange greetings. Mr. Kennedy is talking to Mrs. Lincoln about a photograph she wants inscribed. The President is not always tractable about these eight-by-ten status symbols; the filing cabinets are full of stereotyped likenesses of Mr. Kennedy, and in most cases he considers it a waste of precious time to do more than scribble John F. Kennedy at the bottom. Mrs. Lincoln accepts the inscription, thanks the President, and leaves.

The two men talk for a while on ideas which should be incorporated into a domestic political speech. Sorensen slouches in a chair, his eyes blinking as he listens to the presidential notions. Mr. Kennedy declines the idea of carping on the misdeeds of the Republican Party when it was in power in the United States. He prefers the positive approach of telling the people exactly what his Administration has done for the Republic, and what legislation he proposes to put before the Congress.

Sorensen likes the motif, but thinks it may sound too much like a pre-election speech. "It's too early," he says, and Mr. Kennedy agrees that the talk could be misinterpreted. They talk on, and agree tentatively that the theme should be America Yesterday, Today, and Tomorrow. The speech will be delivered in the Midwest, the area where Mr. Kennedy was weakest in 1960.

Sorensen takes his leave. His role in the White House is difficult and frustrating because it is essentially creative, and no one who makes something out of nothing enjoys the prospect of someone else abusing it. Ted Sorensen and his staff research each subject with care, sparing neither time nor themselves. When the first draft is completed, the President reads it and sometimes turns it down completely. This means that, somehow, the two men failed to communicate with each other at the original conference, and another, and longer, one is scheduled at once.

Sometimes the President accepts the first draft, except for a paragraph or two. Or he may make marginal notes for alterations, deletions, and additional thoughts. Sometimes he calls Salinger, Bundy, and O'Donnell in to read the speech and to listen to objections, approvals, and equivocations.

When Mr. Kennedy came home from the war, he ran for Congress in the Bunker Hill area of Massachusetts. As a speaker, he was so poor that some of his adherents said that they did not mind the hesitations of speech, or even the painful pauses, but the suspicion grew that John F. Kennedy did not know how to end a speech and get offstage. He has come a long way from that. His delivery is firm; his phrasing is so finely honed that some of his utterances will live in history. His New England accent is the butt of comedians' jokes, but the philosophy and impact of his thoughts may some day be perpetuated in granite.

# 10:00 A.M.

J. Bernard West stops in the State Dining Room and watches carpenters hammer the legs of the U-shaped table together. It will not be used until tomorrow, but he must anticipate problems. He flirts a cigarette ash into a tray and beams. "I'm a calm person," he has said. "Nothing ever blows up. Everything goes right. Everything had better go right."

In the reception room of the west wing, Mr. Mitchell, in charge of guests, takes the hat and coat of Secretary of Agriculture Freeman, hangs them properly, and escorts him to the President's office. George Thomas takes some of the President's suits from the family quarters up to his room. Mr. Thomas selects the lulls in his day as the best time for private work. Now he sets his ironing board out, plugs the iron in, gets a smooth damp cloth, and begins to press those Kennedy suits which are in need of fresh creases.

If the suits have spots, George Thomas sends them out to be cleaned. He also sends out all

39

shirts. The President likes a little starch in his collars and cuffs, not enough to make them stiff, but just enough to keep them from wilting on warm days, or in hot rooms. His desire for personal cleanliness is close to an obsession, and the men around him are aware of it.

In the private school, Miss Grimes studies her watch. The children are hunched over their desks, painfully printing words, some doing it carelessly, others grasping the pencil as though to strangle it, some with tongue out caught between teeth. She will wait another two minutes, then ask them to stop writing. At ten-fifteen little hands will be washed at miniature basins, and the children will get their plastic cups from their lockers. Then everyone will drink orange juice and eat cookies.

At the east gate on Pennsylvania Avenue, groups of American citizens stand in line waiting to be admitted to the White House. Some have come a long way for this moment. Others are from nearby states. All have a common emotion —curiosity. They stand chatting, until the White House policeman waves them on; he studies all persons who carry packages and he asks that these things be opened for inspection. A superior officer stands aside and studies the faces in the crowd. An unstable visitor isn't easy to pick out.

The people who clump through the beautiful rooms of the White House are mostly people who would not permit strangers in their homes. Even mannerly strangers. However, they feel that their money, and the money of their ancestors, bought the White House and maintained it, and, as citizens, they have a right to see it, touch it, examine it insofar as the roped-off rooms will permit, and even to snatch a small memento if the guards are not watching. (There are few vandals, however, among the 1,300,000 persons who make the White House tour every year; most people are considerate.) Many visitors have the forlorn hope of catching a glimpse of the President or Mrs. Kennedy.

The White House is a symbol of America only slightly less important than the Capitol. On November 1, 1800, President Adams wrote to his Abigail: "I pray Heaven to bestow the best of Blessings on this House and all that shall hereafter inhabit it. May none but honest and wise Men ever rule under this roof."

The entrance to the White House is in perpetual dispute. When James Hoban designed the original building, he made it a double-entrance house, with an ornate portico on the Pennsylvania Avenue side, and an even more imposing one on the south side, facing the President's Park. The White House police department, which numbers 204 men, is almost equally divided about which side represents the "front entrance" to the house.

President Abraham Lincoln had meats and groceries delivered on the south side, so he must have thought of Pennsylvania Avenue as being "the front door." Almost every president in the twentieth century has welcomed chiefs of state on the Pennsylvania Avenue (north side), but honored guests are asked to report at the south-side reception room. Politicians and friends who want to see the President are checked through the west gate; those who have appointments with Mrs. Kennedy, Arthur Schlesinger, historian and advisor to the President, the military aides, and the Secret Service are escorted through the east gate.

The question of the number of floors in the White House can lead to a lively discussion. The sixty-odd acres of greensward on which the mansion sits slope from north to south, from Pennsylvania Avenue down toward South Executive Avenue. Thus, what appears to be the ground floor from Pennsylvania Avenue, is actually the second floor when seen from the south side. Almost everyone who has seen the White House from outside the fence is sure that it is a two-story building with long one-story annexes stretching away from it on both sides.

The White House is divided into three parts: the mansion, the east wing and the west wing. The ground floor and first floor of the mansion consist of public rooms; the second floor—at least part of it—is where the First Family lives. The third floor is divided among servants' quarters and the school. The wings stretch away from the mansion on either side. The east wing, as noted before, is divided into offices for the First Lady's official family, the Secret Service, Arthur Schlesinger, the White House police, and three military aides. The other wing—the westerly one—contains the President's office and those of his assistants, and includes a press room and a swimming pool.

The history of the mansion is, at best, haphazard. The cornerstone was laid by President George Washington on October 13, 1792. He is the only President who did not live in it. The John Adams family moved in in the autumn of 1800, and Mrs. Adams used the big East Room for drying the family wash. Fourteen years later the British burned it when they took the city in the War of 1812.

The White House was over a hundred years old when Theodore Roosevelt called it a conglomeration of styles and periods, set in a building which was structurally dangerous to its occupants. Congress appropriated $500,000 to repair it, but the foundation was still too weak to support the building, and the strain on the main timbers was so great that the floors and ceilings actually bowed.

It was not until the early part of the second Truman Administration that Congress decided to make the White House the strikingly beautiful place it could be. In December, 1949, the Harry Truman family moved to Blair House, and more than $5,000,000 was spent taking everything out of the mansion except the outer walls. Steel girders replaced ancient wooden bowed beams, and concrete was poured to support the old foundations. The old sandstone walls, which were quarried in nearby Virginia in 1796, were maintained intact, and the work of refitting the interior—with its oak parquet, cornices, and columns —became the most difficult task. Even so, deeper excavating provided more space, and a mansion which at one time had sixty-two rooms and fourteen baths now has one hundred thirty-two rooms and twenty baths.

Kenneth O'Donnell looks at his watch. He stands with his back to the door leading to the President's office. He is talking to Dave Powers, the Boston Bully Boy. "Freeman has been in there thirteen minutes," O'Donnell says. "I'll give him one more."

Powers, who is concerned with practically everything the President does, asks, "What's the best method you've found for getting them out of there?"

O'Donnell turns on his broad lipless grin. "When I think the time is up," he answers, "I just walk in. Usually the visitor takes the hint and says good-bye to the President."

"Suppose," says Powers, "that the President wants to talk a little more with the Secretary of Agriculture, or whoever it is?"

O'Donnell shakes his head. "Then," he says, "the President looks up at me frowning. As soon as I see it, I duck out, and try again five minutes later."

Powers thinks it is a good system.

"Did I ever tell you," Powers says musingly, "about when he came home from the war and ran for Congress?" O'Donnell nods. "I was living in a walk-up flat in Charlestown, and one night there's a knock on the door—this is 1946, mind you—and I open the door. The landlord has a twenty-watt bulb in the hall and I can't see who the man is. It's Jack Kennedy, and he says he's running for Congress in the Bunker Hill district and will I help him. Well, of course I'll help him, and I invite him in and we talk about it.

"I set it up for him to make a speech to the Gold Star Mothers, and you never in your life heard such a speech. He's hemming and hawing and you'd need a pair of pliers to drag the next sentence out of him. The women are all sitting there, waiting to hear him say something, and very little is coming out. Worse than that, it looks like he never learned how to end a speech. It's going on and on and I'm beginning to perspire.

"All of a sudden he says it. The right words come to him and he says it. He says: 'Well, I think I know how you ladies feel. My mother, too, lost a son in the war.' Ken, you never saw anything like it. They broke into applause; some

45

of them started to cry, and the mothers rushed forward to grab his hand and hug him. That was his first campaign, and from that minute onward, you could see the tide turn his way."

O'Donnell is still smiling. "He's come a long way." With the speaking too, says Powers.

O'Donnell excuses himself and goes into the President's office. In a moment he is out again, chatting with the Secretary of Agriculture. One more minute and he escorts Angier Biddle Duke into the President's office. Mr. Duke, of the Philadelphia Biddle-Dukes, is the State Department executive in charge of protocol. When distinguished foreign statesmen visit the United States, it is Mr. Duke's chore to check off the minutes, the places, the people, so that every part of the visit is pleasing, not only to the statesman-guest, but to the President too.

In years past, the State Department used to roll a red carpet through Union Station, and the president waited, in high hat and cutaway, to greet the incoming train. But times change. In the Roosevelt and Truman Administrations the visitor came in at Washington National Airport, and the president waited at the foot of an airplane ramp. In the Eisenhower Administration the same policy was continued, except that the locale was sometimes Andrews Field, and on cold days, Mr. Eisenhower and State Secretary Dulles appeared to wear faces frozen rigid.

The helicopter, and Mr. Kennedy's evaluation of time, changed the welcome again. Now the visitor is first brought to Williamsburg, a town of historic interest restored to its eighteenth-century elegance, and there the king, or president, or prime minister rests overnight from his journey. In the morning he and his party are flown by helicopters to the south lawn of the White House, to a place between the great fountain and the south drive, and there the visitors are met by Mr. Duke.

Outside the south White House portico, a red rug is laid between the ground-floor diplomats' reception room and a small dais on the lawn. The visitors are brought two hundred yards by car; the President, notified in his office five minutes before the helicopters land, leaves through the French doors, walks to the red rug, and, with Dean Rusk, awaits the convoy of automobiles. Members of the embassy of the country involved stand in a receiving line with their names in white pasted to the concrete walk. Television and newsreel cameras are in readiness; so are the White House correspondents and such distinguished Americans as may be invited to the ceremony.

A twenty-one-gun salute is fired in the park— aimed away from the White House. On the main-floor portico the Marine Band plays the national anthems of both countries; Mr. Duke makes the proper introductions and enunciates the proper

47

words. The receiving line is kept short, because the President of the United States does not like long ones. In fact, the entire procedure—while necessary and traditionally respectful—is a waste of time as far as the President is concerned. In many cases, he feels this way about state luncheons and dinners too. Mr. Kennedy would much prefer to meet chiefs of state face-to-face in the office and sit down to the business at hand—guarantees of peace, the enhancement of trade, mutual aid, or friendly accord between nations. One of the gifts from Mr. Kennedy to the visiting chief of state is usually a color motion picture of the welcoming ceremony. The President frets when he must sit and watch this with his distinguished guest.

At ten forty-two Pierre Salinger is in, and Mr. Duke is out. The press secretary is a former newspaper and magazine editor who wears his experience at a rakish angle. Cigars are a feature of his face, and he walks in with the gait of a humpty-dumpty doll which may be knocked down but which will bounce upright automatically. "Good morning, Mr. President," he says. He sits with pencil and notebook and listens as President Kennedy primes him for the Salinger press conference at eleven. They go over the fresh news together, and they go over the follow-up news of yesterday.

Salinger makes a few suggestions. The President thinks for a moment, and either accepts or rejects them. They discuss the official calendar for today, and the portents of these visits. They anticipate the questions which may be asked during the daily press conference. In ten minutes Salinger takes his leave and returns to his office with his notes.

On the south lawn, the schoolchildren are in recess. Some play on the big canvas trampoline; a few are on the swings. One climbs up into the little tree hut. Two girls are inside an oversized doll house playing mamma. In spite of their youth they realize that no doll house is big enough for two mammas, and this leads to a few acrimonious words.

Miss Grimes stands aside, arms folded, watching the children at play. She makes certain that the sweaters are on, and buttoned. The sun is high and the small breeze has died in increasing warmth. Suddenly she hears three faint claps of hands. Miss Grimes turns. There, standing in the French doors of his office, is the President. After Pierre Salinger left he had been about to make a phone call when he heard the childish yells. His signal for attention is always the same: three loud claps.

The youngsters know it. They stop play. Led by Caroline Kennedy, they race for the White House. For a moment or two this man is not the President of the United States. He is just another father trying to enjoy the company of children without appearing to be condescending. He crouches low in the doorway, talks as excitedly about the games as the children do, and points to the workmen on the lawn with their blowing machines, forcing the dead leaves into piles. Soon, he says, there may be snow and can you imagine how much fun we'll have then?

The mere suggestion of snow, and snowballs, and sleighriding down the slopes of the lawn is enough to make all of them squeal, and they run off.

# 11:00 A.M.

There is a canopy over the west wing. Outside of it, television and motion-picture cameras are set up almost perpetually, since distinguished visitors —even congressional leaders—use this entrance to get to the President's office. Inside the door is a small hallway leading to a large reception room. On the right side of the hall are the phone booths of the reporters, with direct lines to their wire services and newspapers. On the left side is a squarish room jammed with typewriters, papers, and the debris of the inquiring mind. Next to this office is a smaller one for the Secret Service men who are on duty in the executive wing.

The big reception room is dominated by the Philippine table. It is a huge, circular object with carved legs featuring the heads of water buffaloes. The top, which by itself would fill a small dining room, was cut from a single mahogany tree in one slice. Time and the lack of proper humidity in the White House press reception room have caused a jagged crack to break across the surface, but it still holds the hats and canes of dapper diplomats, the cameras and coats of press photographers, the impedimenta of reporters, and the briefcases of Cabinet members.

Once, during the war, when Aguinaldo of the Philippines defected to the Japanese, the big table was removed and hidden in storage. When the war was over, and Manila was again a free city with a free government, the table was brought back and set up in its center spot. Around the walls of the room are new black sofas and chairs, positioned beneath the frowns and stares of past presidents.

Christine Camp comes out of the Salinger office and summons the press. Some follow her at leisure, others hurry. The word passes around the press room, and reporters sipping coffee place the containers on desks, grab pencils and papers, and run. In the little hall, Merriman Smith, dean of the White House press corps, steps into a phone booth and says: "The press conference is about to begin. I'll be back in a few minutes."

Salinger sits behind his desk puffing and leaning back toward shelves of books and political cartoons, waiting for the last journalist to arrive. Then he stands. Three stenographers are in the room, two against the walls and one before his desk. They take notes, so that if there is a dispute about what Salinger told the press, the exact words can be typed up and compared with what the press has reported.

There have been, of course, considerable differences in press secretaries. Joseph Tumulty, secretary to Woodrow Wilson, felt that the work of a president was, by nature, a secret not to be revealed. Louis McHenry Howe of Franklin D. Roosevelt's staff used the press for political purposes, and, in the first term, played the newspapers as a concertmaster might play a mighty organ. Matt Connolly of Truman's staff treated "the boys" as though they were all friends. James Hagerty regarded one and all with suspicion, and traded sarcasm with them. Salinger is jolly, offhand, but, when the occasion requires it, tough. Sometimes, in the late afternoon, his phone calls with editors often sound like this: "No . . . you're wrong. . . . I don't care where you got it, you're wrong. . . . Nothing like that is in the works here. . . . Listen: I don't know where you get your leaks, but I'd suggest that you find a new one."

At this press conference he makes his announcements fast and brief, pausing only when asked for background material or how a name is spelled: "President saw Secretary of Agriculture ten o'clock. They talked about corn surpluses. No decisions made. No story yet. The President also saw Angier Biddle Duke on a matter of the state visit tomorrow. Arrangements were discussed. He also saw some of his assistants, including Ted

Sorensen. Nothing exciting. You have all seen the day's calendar. Unless something unusual breaks, it will be a routine day."

Someone says: "Does the President have any comment on—"

Salinger says: "None."

The reporters laugh.

"Excuse me," Salinger says. "I was joking."

"Does the President have any comment on last night's speech by Mao Tse-tung?"

Salinger rolls the cigar around in his mouth. "The one about how we ought to dismantle our nuclear weapons?" he asks, smiling. "No comment."

"How about the new budget, Pierre?" someone says with an edge of irritation.

Salinger shrugs. "When the President receives the report of his budget director, he will have comment. Probably plenty. But the budget is not finalized and—"

"My office says it's going to be three billion over last year," the reporter says.

"In that case," Salinger says, "your office knows more than the President at this stage, because we have no news at all."

"What about that tax cut?"

"Why ask here? Tax cuts are suggested by the President, but they are made on Capitol Hill."

"Does the President think he will take the Southern states this time?"

"He'll be trying. Let's put it that way."

"Will the President go to Palm Beach again this year?"

"It's doubtful. It's late in the season and there's a campaign coming up, I hear. Anything else?"

There is nothing else. It is a dull day, far below the average in activity, in spot news, in general excitement. "You know about the signing of the health bill in the Cabinet Room?" Salinger asks. The reporters nod as they write. "In twenty minutes," Salinger says. "I'll have Chris call you in plenty of time. Cameras and lights will be set on the near side of the table. The President will be the only person seated at the signing."

"That's the mental retardation thing," a reporter says.

"Right," says Salinger.

The reporters file out. The three stenographers take their notes and leave the room.

Salinger begins to examine his mail. Miss Camp comes to his desk and watches. He riffles slowly, like a disillusioned card player. He makes guttural comments on some, comments understood only by Christine Camp. "Are the photographers set up?" he asks. Yes. They are in the Cabinet Room and they are ready. Salinger looks at his watch. "Give the President about three minutes," he says. "Then call the reporters in."

He gets to his feet and walks out the corridor

and down the hall to the presidential office. Mrs. Kennedy is there with young John. Salinger starts out of the office but the President waves him back in. The First Lady says that she came back a little early because she's going to visit her mother this afternoon, and there are some things she wants to do first.

The President holds his arms out. "John-John," he says happily, "tell me a secret." John knows the ritual well, and he runs toward his father and whispers a buzzing sound. The President leans back in his great chair with a good imitation of wide-eyed surprise. "You . . . don't . . . tell . . . me!" he says. Little John laughs heartily and runs around the desk. When he gets to the front of it, he pushes hard against the panel holding the Seal of the United States, swings it inward, and disappears inside his father's desk.

The child is fetched, protesting a little, from the desk and leaves with his mother. They go out through the French doors and down the colonnaded walk to the mansion. In a few minutes Mrs. Kennedy is upstairs phoning Mr. West about some changes she would like to have made in the State Dining Room. She is always considerate of employees. She has the rare talent of extending cordiality to them and to servants without inducing familiarity on their part. As she talks, she is suggesting changes in the shape of the table, and she asks for additional lighting in the big room. Little John is now in the care of Miss Shaw, but he runs from her and, at top speed, swings around his mother's knees as she speaks to the chief usher.

# NOON

In the west wing, the reception room is busy. Vice-President Lyndon Johnson passes through, dropping his hat and coat on the Philippine table. Behind him is Anthony Celebrezze, Secretary of Health, Education and Welfare, and Senator Abraham Ribicoff. Others walk through—a congressional representative who introduced the bill about to be signed, Mrs. Sargent Shriver, the President's sister, who walks through Salinger's office, a few under secretaries, Senator Clinton Anderson, and some doctors.

All are ushered into the Cabinet Room. It is an oblong room, large and somber. The titles of the various secretaries are on metal plates on the back of the black leather chairs. The table is boat-shaped. The President, instead of sitting at the head of it, will sit in the center with his back to the French doors. In the table are electrical plugs reading "English" and "Other." No president has called fewer Cabinet meetings than this one.

There were only six in the first three years of the Kennedy Administration.

President Eisenhower called a Cabinet meeting almost every Friday of his eight years in office. Most other presidents, including Lincoln, solicited the collective intelligence of the men in the highest government posts, but Mr. Kennedy prefers solitary expert opinion, so he calls the man most involved and most knowledgeable and confers with him alone, or in concert with McGeorge Bundy and one or two others of the White House assistants. In this way Mr. Kennedy does not have to listen to interminable opinions from men not directly concerned.

The officers of the government line up behind the President's chair. They stand. On the other side of the table flood lights are turned on and cameras are focused on the important chair. The additional lights make the rug look greener, the walls creamier in tone. From the wall, Thomas Jefferson studies the scene with the urbanity of a gentleman not easily impressed.

The President comes in. He smiles to those on both sides of the table, pauses to whisper something to his sister, and proceeds directly to his big chair. His suit is blue; his thick hair has coppery tints; the smile is strong and winning. If his back hurts, no one will know. He leans back to listen to something the Vice-President is saying, and he laughs.

Before him as he sits down is the congressional bill which will become law when he signs it. He stares seriously into the camera lenses across the table and, when he hears them begin to whir, he speaks. The bill, he says, is the first, he hopes, of many which will help retarded children. The federal government, until now, has contributed nothing in this area. He hopes that several states will follow suit with bills of their own. Until recently mental retardation was regarded as incurable, but science, he says, has learned much and now a great deal can be done to help the young.

The speech is short and direct. He hides his impatience to return to his work. On the right side of the desk blotter is a holder with twenty pens. In turn, he dips each one in an ink well, squiggles a small part of his signature, and stops to present the pen to an interested party. The importance of the presidential pen as a memento started with Franklin D. Roosevelt. Roosevelt, however, wrote his signature with one pen—in his first term—and gave it to the representative or senator who fathered the bill in question. Later he used two or three pens. Truman followed the practice; so did Eisenhower.

When the last part of the letter *y* in Kennedy is written, the President stands, smiling, smooths his jacket down, reaches inside and tugs his tie down, and walks back to his office. The newsmen pack their gear and leave. Some of the politicians remain a few minutes; some merely reach for Mr. Kennedy's hand as he passes.

He goes back through Mrs. Lincoln's office to his own. With him is Douglas Dillon, Secretary of the Treasury. Mr. Kennedy wants an up-to-date briefing on the drainage of gold from the United States Treasury. The President stands close to the French door where the floor is marked by Eisenhower's golf spikes, and the two men talk for a minute or two. The spending of American dollars abroad is of deep concern to these men. It is spent by a million tourists, and it is spent by servicemen and their families who live in foreign countries. One of the wry jokes around the White House is that if the United States finds itself short of cash, the Federal Republic of Germany will lend it to us.

Mr. Dillon reports that the problem is being brought under control in stages. The drain of gold is decreasing, but it is obvious that the President would like to find a way of cutting it abruptly, so that the United States would at least be able to maintain its solid fiscal position among the Western nations, or even improve it.

# 1:00 P.M.

---

The last of the public visitors to the White House has been checked out. The roped-off areas of the ground floor and first floor are again open. Mr. West sits in his little office, idly flicking a fly swatter. He is engrossed in a small cardboard representation of the state dining table for tomorrow. Small canoe-shaped cards are stuck in place around the table. Mr. West blinks behind his glasses as he studies the layout.

The white cards represent male guests; the blue are female. Each one bears a name in dark ink. The one red card bears the President's name. The fly swatter flicks slowly toward the desk, taps a paper and lifts again. Mr. West holds his cigarette away from his face. He calls an assistant and points to the places where he wants the flowers to be. Then he phones Nancy Tuckerman and tells her that he has studied the new layout and has directed the carpenters to fashion the table in the specified design.

Mr. West is a philosopher. "I just do as I am

62

told," he tells his assistant. "We all do around here." He sets the swatter down and studies a brown paper package tied with white string. On it is a legend: "The Robert Kennedy Children clothes from Camp David."

The chief usher's staff consists of about seventy persons. There are thirty-five servants, including a head chef, an assistant head chef who cooks for the Kennedy family, five butlers who are actually waiters, five maids, one pantry girl, two laundresses, and five housemen who clean the state floors; thirty-five others are in the maintenance section—carpenters, plumbers, engineers, painters, electricians, flower arrangers, and five doormen.

Mr. West is also charged with the upkeep of the storeroom in the basement. If, for example, a hundred extra chairs are needed for a concert in the East Room, it is his duty to see that someone is assigned to get them and that others will place them in the room according to Mrs. Kennedy's wishes. The President has little to say about the day-to-day administration of the mansion itself. Whatever notions he may have, he communicates to his wife, who relays them to Mr. West.

When he isn't busy, the chief usher becomes what he calls "a friendly spy." He walks around the mansion, from floor to floor, from room to room, his eyes rarely missing a drape hanging askew, or a cook lounging when onions should be peeled, or a film of dust on a fireplace mantel. In spite of the importance of his position, Mr. West is not a voice-raiser; his tone is soft and assuring. He can arouse the cook to peeling onions merely by bowing slightly and saying: "Hello"; a houseman will rush to a dusty mantel with a cloth if Mr. West so much as flicks the top of it with his index finger.

In the school, Miss Grimes leads the class in prayer. It does not matter that the Supreme Court frowns upon it; the prayer is said as a thanksgiving to God for lunch. The children get their plastic cups for their milk and then open their lunchboxes. Caroline Kennedy, of course, lives in the house, but Mrs. Kennedy will not permit her to join the family at lunch because it would be a privilege denied to the other students, so she too opens her lunchbox. Now, in the relaxed chatter of children who enjoy eating and talking at the same time, the small classroom sounds like an aviary.

The milk for the children is furnished by the White House, but it is paid for by each student as part of his tuition. In each lunchbox is a sandwich and some fruit. Jerry Behn, the chief of the White House Secret Service, walks up the ramp to the class, sticks his head in, nods at the happy talk, and leaves, making the rounds of the mansion to see that everything is in order. And everyone, too.

In the west wing, McGeorge Bundy walks into

Ken O'Donnell's office and says that he would like to see the President at once. O'Donnell makes the request. In a moment Bundy is inside. The President has been reading some of the newspapers stacked on a table behind his desk. He puts them aside and asks his assistant to be seated. The news is that Premier Khrushchev has just made another "soft line" speech in Moscow, one which indicates that the Russians feel that world peace can be maintained by the Soviet Union and the United States acting in co-operation with each other. The speech was intercepted by United States listening posts, and arrived on the Situation Room teletype three minutes ago. Bundy hands the tape to the President, who reads it with interest.

This place, which is down a short flight of stairs from Bundy's office on the ground floor, is correctly referred to as the International Situation Area. In it are teletypes from the Associated Press, Reuters, and United Press International; classified machines from the Central Intelligence Agency and the Department of Defense, as well as a map room and conference table. The machines supply, continually, reports of events in foreign lands and from America. The intelligence machines decipher, decode, listen, evaluate, and tell.

The wall maps can be covered or exposed. They show the disposition of United States forces everywhere in the world. If the Seventh Fleet moves out of the Formosa Straits for any reason, the fact can be seen at a glance on the map. If an Army unit is transferred by aircraft from Puerto Rico to West Germany, it is a statistic on a board. The President can speak directly to De Gaulle of France, Erhard of Germany, or Home of Britain. All he has to do is place a highly secret index card into the telephone, and the connection is made at once. The personage receiving the call must also place the right coded card into his telephone, or he will not receive it. The voices, of course, are scrambled so that no one else can intercept the words.

When the hot line running between President Kennedy and Premier Khrushchev was ready, it was set up in the Pentagon rather than in the White House. Messages for the President are passed through the office of the Secretary of Defense, and then on to the President by direct wire. It is not a telephone. It is really two teletype machines, one of which prints in Russian, the other in English. Last autumn, when they were ready, both sides decided to test them for accuracy. After the first American trial, Moscow sent a query: "Please explain what is meant by a quick brown fox jumping over a lazy dog."

The President finishes reading the intercepted speech. His attitude is cautious. "What does C.I.A. think of it?" . . . "Have you got anything from

Kohler yet?" (Foy Kohler is the United States Ambassador to the Soviet Union.) ... "How much of this do you discount?" ... "They're still doing business with Fidel, aren't they?" Mr. Kennedy thinks of calling Mr. Rusk and Mr. McNamara in to discuss the friendliness of the Russian tone in the light of the Soviet's long-term antagonism toward the United States. He decides not to do it—at least not before lunch—because he wants Ambassador Kohler's opinion and the views of Mr. McCone of C.I.A.

Often, when the matter is more important than today's speech, the President calls an emergency meeting of the National Security Council. When this happens, the reporters in the press room scan the faces inbound to try to discover the gravity of the situation. The faces belong to McCone, Bundy, Robert Kennedy, General Maxwell Taylor, Rusk, McNamara, and, sometimes, Edward R. Murrow.

The nation's safety, in a sense, devolves upon the deliberations of these men. In another sense, it does not, because after these men have given President Kennedy their best opinions, he is the one who makes the decision. Sometimes, when the President finds himself in accord with these men, he will play the devil's advocate and take the opposite side of the question merely to see if he can support it with logic. No one can recall a time when he found himself opposed to the six who attend all Security Council sessions, but no one doubts that if he was in this awkward position, the President would give all hands a chance to alter his thinking, but if they failed, he would pursue his course.

The President is a fighter, a man who respects his intellect and is willing to follow its conclusions. He is conscious of the presidency at all times and is confident that he will go down in history as a good chief executive. When a Cabinet member makes an error—and this applies also to his valued assistants—he can become loud and caustic. No one is ever in doubt about who is boss around the White House, and no one except his old friends ever refers to him as anything but "Mr. President." Nevertheless he does court honest disagreement. Anyone can tell Mr. Kennedy that he is wrong in an assumption, a directive, or a course of action—but the assertion must be backed by documented facts. The President has been known to alter a proposed course of action when his subordinates have convinced him that he is wrong. If they can't do this, he issues his orders exactly as planned.

On the other hand, he represses his irritation in the presence of men he does not trust. He treats them coolly, civilly, and ignores poor opinions with a polite nod. There is reason to believe that inwardly he likes to consider himself as hard. Sometimes he quotes an old aphorism coined by

Knute Rockne of Notre Dame: "When the going gets tough, the tough get going."

It is one-fifteen, and school is out. Caroline waves good-bye to her classmates and joins her mother on the second floor. They talk about schoolwork for a moment, the mother with an arm around her daughter. Caroline rehearses the fundamental French she studied for the maternal approval it might warrant. Little John comes out of his bathroom nude, running at top speed down the hall with a flag on a long staff.

Mrs. Kennedy holds her hand against her mouth and murmurs: "Oh my God!" The wild running in circles and the nudity bring a smile, but Mrs. Kennedy tries to be stern. "You go back into your bath, Johnny-Wonny." He turns without answering, and runs through the door to his bedroom with the flag held high over his head. The flagstaff jams across the doorway, but he keeps running as it falls to the floor. The little body leaps into the tub while Miss Shaw sits beside it, waiting for the big splash.

A few minutes later Mrs. Kennedy puts both children to bed. (She often has lunch with John before his nap.) There are no reprieves at naptime.

The President calls for Dave Powers. The relationship between the two is warm and personal. When Mrs. Kennedy is away from the White House, or when the President is on a political tour, Powers is at his side almost all the time. It is begging the issue to say that Dave Powers knows the President's mind, knows whom he will see and whom he will not; Mr. Powers has a personal joke that covers the situation: "My family calls me John's other wife."

Powers has the friendliness, the zeal, and the political perspicacity of the second-generation Irish who have worked on the ward level. He knows what it is like to live in a third-floor walk-up flat, and, what is more important, he is unafraid to remember it. Or to return to it. His country, his family, his church, and John F. Kennedy are his work and his life, and he can spin yarns about any or all of these with such dry and wry humor that Ken O'Donnell and the President often break into a grin at the mere sight of Powers walking through the office.

Still, he is no court jester, no buffoon. His merchandise is his memory. Powers has learned a great deal about life and people through experience, and he has forgotten none of it, including the dates. His political horizons have lifted beyond the shallow confines of Charlestown and Bunker Hill to the national level, and he finds it as easy to recall what happened to John F. Kennedy in Minnesota or Montana as in Massachusetts.

The President is signing mail. Mrs. Lincoln stands at the desk, taking the letters one by one. "Let's go, Dave," the President says. He stands and the two men leave the office. They walk out through the French doors into the sunshine. The President moves smartly under the colonnades toward the swimming pool, an indoor one lying between the office and the mansion. It was installed in the early days of Franklin D. Roosevelt's Administration and was used for the proper exercise of his afflicted limbs.

Mr. Kennedy is devoted to the use of the swimming pool. He is in it twice a day—just before lunch, and again prior to dinner. The two men pass a White House policeman, and, directly ahead, a Secret Service man opens the door to the exercise room. Mr. Kennedy stops a moment to look at the hedged-in rose garden. The signature of Mrs. Kennedy is beginning to appear on many parts of the White House, and here too she has left her mark. The garden—which is the President's—is now alight with zinnias in whites, reds, and rust, backed by the inclined heads of roses.

"It's beginning to look nice," the President says, and walks into the gymnasium. Powers follows. As the President sheds his clothing, so too he sheds the cares of his position. Wrinkled swim trunks hang on pegs. There are weights and pulleys against the wall, a scale, and a massage table.

Mr. Kennedy tugs the trunks up, walks into the other room, and slips into the pool. He comes to the surface, flicks his thick hair back, and swims up and back the fifty-foot length twice in silence. He keeps himself in good physical condition, and like all the Kennedys, is conscious of the importance of exercise. Dave gets in the pool, and moves slowly toward the middle. He uses a breast stroke, because he says it is the only way in which a man can swim and talk at the same time.

The room is not large. It is about sixty feet by twenty-five, and the swimming pool occupies fifty-by-twenty of this. The outer wall is blue-mirrored. On the remaining three, the President had an artist paint a floor-to-ceiling mural of a Massachusetts waterfront, complete with bays, schooners and launches at anchor, Cape Cod houses, and trees.

Along the base of the walls hang round life preservers. These are souvenirs, marked: "USS *Oriskany* CVA 34" and "USS *J. P. Kennedy, Jr.* DD 850." There is a red telephone on a pillow at the edge of the pool. The President of the United States is never more than a few feet from a telephone, whether he is in the swimming pool, in his Boeing jet, in bed, or in an automobile. He is in a position at all times to make instantaneous decisions—even if that decision involves nuclear war.

The temperature of the pool is maintained at ninety degrees, too warm for most swimmers but good for those who swim for its therapeutic value. The two men engage in light talk as they swim.

Sometimes it embraces sports; at other times, it's an amusing family story, or a funny one that Dave remembers from the days when James Curley was running Boston and Massachusetts. The New England tones of the men ricochet off the walls of the room, and the President appears to draw as much good from the recollections of Dave Powers as he does from his swim.

Mr. Kennedy is in no hurry to leave. He usually remains in the pool for forty minutes, or, more precisely, thirty minutes in the pool and ten minutes undressing and dressing. His muscular structure is firm and strong, and except for the chronic backache, he could participate in most sports today.

# 2:00 P.M.

The two men part on the colonnade. The President takes a folder of work with him. Dave Powers returns to his office. A Secret Service man falls into step beside the President and they walk into the mansion. Mr. Kennedy is not made conscious of it, but his exact whereabouts are clocked at all times. When he leaves the pool, the word is flashed from Mrs. Lincoln's office to other offices in the executive wing. "The President has just left the pool for the mansion."

In their quarters, Mr. and Mrs. Kennedy eat lunch from trays. They are served grilled-cheese sandwiches, or cold beef, often with cups of consommé. The President drinks tea, or a glass of milk. His practice is to have coffee only in the morning. They chat about family matters, never about matters of state. The President does not usually talk about his work at home. Once, in the third year of the Kennedy Administration, Jacqueline Kennedy idly asked her husband what kind of a day it was.

It was the first time she'd asked such a broad question, and she never asked it again. The President shook his head negatively, and, holding his hand up, ticked off ten things which had gone wrong throughout the morning. "And," he said, "the day is only half over."

Even a simple lunch together means more to the Kennedys than it would to most other couples. She husbands the hours they spend together, and she guards the sanctuary of the second floor as though one moment of relaxed vigilance would bring hordes of politicians tramping through the rooms. Her strong opinions—independent of her husband's—make her treasure old friends rather than new; make her assess public figures as self-seeking politicians rather than as public servants. She looks forward to trips abroad or to various retreats as a means of escaping life under a glass bell.

Her husband, on the other hand, rarely expresses concern about keeping his public and private life separate. He renders unto the United States all the time and devotion and effort he can give it—his average workday, in the office and at home, comes to fourteen hours—and he tries to spend all the time that is left with his wife and children, because he too aspires to a normal family life. The work schedule of any president is lengthy and enervating, and it makes its demands seven days a week every week, but Mr. Kennedy knows that he must make the time for his wife and children. And he seems to have no trouble doing so. If there is any difference between their married life now and the way it was before, it is that Mrs. Kennedy finds her husband becoming more of a home man—as happened to his father a long time ago. Joseph P. Kennedy reached a stage—before his illness—where he desired most of all to be home surrounded by his wife and his children. The President, as time goes on, reminds Mrs. Kennedy more and more of his father.

When lunch is over, a silent period engulfs the second floor. Mrs. Kennedy uses this part of the day to paint, or to take a nap. The President goes to his bedroom with his papers. George Thomas draws the drapes and says: "Mr. President, what time do you want me to call you?" Mr. Kennedy says: "Three-thirty, George." He undresses, and drops on the bed. A night light enables him to read the papers he has brought with him, and he makes marginal notations. He does not work long. After a few minutes the papers are tossed on a chair, the light is snapped off, and the President stretches out on the bed, eyes closed.

It is a superficial nap, a dozing which permits vague images to cross the mind, and allows the ears to pick up the thunder of a jet coming up out of Washington International Airport. The President is not sufficiently fatigued to fall into deep sleep. Besides, his mind is alert to the problems of his office, and whether he wills it or not, they ride the mental carousel as they do with other mortals. Still, there is relaxation, a midday lassitude which permeates the second floor.

The living section of the mansion is not pretty. It is makeshift, a potpourri of rooms which do not relate to any whole. When President Eisenhower was asked where he ate when there were no state dinners, he said: "We eat in the hall." There is a broad corridor which traverses the second floor, running parallel to Pennsylvania Avenue. The west portion of the hall is sealed off by a wall with a door. Thus the presidential sitting room is really part of the corridor, and it was here that President Eisenhower, Mrs. Eisenhower, and Mrs. Dowd often ate dinner while looking at television.

The Kennedys use it as their living room (they call it the West Hall), and Mrs. Kennedy has made it look comfortable with sofas and wing chairs and coffee tables, family photos, and two cupboards of books. There is also a large desk, covered with school papers belonging to Caroline, and a tea cart. There is but one source of natural light, the windows to the west.

On the left side of this living room (as you face the windows) there are two doors: one leads to Mrs. Kennedy's bedroom; the other is to the smaller bedroom used by the President when Mrs. Kennedy is away (he also uses it for breakfast, for important incoming and outgoing phone calls,

and for the perusal of pending bills and schedules). On the right side, a door leads to the family
dining room, one of the loveliest rooms in the
White House. Adjoining it is a kitchen.

Leaving the living room through the partition
which creates it, the children's rooms are on the
right. Across the hall is the Oval Room, with its
beautiful yellow rug and bright paintings. The
corridor floor tilts upward, although no one can
think of an architectural reason for it. There is a
piano in the hall; and moving farther east is the
Lincoln sitting room, where the sixteenth president did much of his daily work, and, next to it,
the famous Lincoln bedroom with its huge dark
rosewood bed.

A large bedroom on the north side, facing
Pennsylvania Avenue, is referred to as "the
Queen's Room" because Her Majesty Queen
Elizabeth used it during her stay in Washington.
Adjoining it is a blue dressing room. Across the
hall is the famous Treaty Room, decorated in
green.

Of all the one hundred and thirty-two rooms in
the White House, the President and his immediate family are, in a sense, restricted to the sitting
room made out of the hall, five bedrooms, a dining room, and a kitchen. When guests of the
President visit the White House, they occupy the
famous rooms at the other end of the hall, where
Lincoln and Queen Elizabeth slept.

George Thomas is back in Room 324 on the third floor. He will wait until a little after three, then he will go to the second floor and tiptoe around the room as he picks up laundry. Mrs. Lincoln is back at her desk. She uses an electric typewriter and her fingers fly as White House messengers come in, leave a package or an envelope without a word, and walk quietly out.

Pierre Salinger is back in his office, puffing on a cigar and making terse notes about the questions he thinks the reporters will ask the President at the four o'clock press conference. The President does not hold regular press conferences, because, as other presidents learned, a few journalists use this period to make anti-Administration speeches calculated to sound like innocent questions.

At first the President went even further than the others. Mr. Kennedy agreed not only to hold regular press conferences but to permit live television coverage. The President had confidence in his ability to fence with the questions and questioners. But he, like his predecessors, found it to be a trial. He plans fewer and fewer press conferences as time goes on. Stubbornly, the President still schedules a few, and he asks no man to submit the questions first, nor does he ask mercy when a few veer away from current topics to ask the baited question—the so-called "curve."

# 3:00 P.M.

On the ground-floor area, McGeorge Bundy has
received an opinion from Ambassador Kohler in
Moscow regarding Mr. Khrushchev's friendly
speech. Mr. Kohler attaches little importance to
it, and reminds the State Department that such
statements, combined with bellicose threats, con-
stitute the Soviet surface policy. He is certain that
the tossing of olive branches to the United States
will be followed by the spitting of olive pits.

The Secretary of State agrees with his ambassador. W. Averell Harriman is also in accord. Major
General C. V. Clifton, the President's military
aide, makes a similar assessment. Mr. Bundy
knows that the President is dozing, and will not
disturb him with a negative finding. However, he
writes a note and sends it to Mrs. Lincoln, to be
drawn to the attention of Mr. Kennedy. After he
dispatches it, word comes in from Mr. McCone
that he too sees nothing new in the Khrushchev
speech.

Bundy and Clifton have an appointment with

the President at three forty-five, and if there is to be further discussion, it will come just before the press conference. In the interim, Bundy proceeds with his normal tasks. He works in the rear of the ground floor, surrounded by stenographers. His office has blue wallpaper, a beige carpet, and a couch; he likes to sip coffee and dwell upon all the things Mr. Kennedy will ask, and try to have replies ready.

Like the C.I.A. and the State Department, he seeks accurate information. Often he gets knowledge from them. Wherever it comes from, it is Bundy's job to get it and to bring it to the attention of his boss at once. He will make the same inquiry of the number-two men in the State Department, the C.I.A., the Defense Department, in addition to the ambassador in the particular country involved. Some of his problems are chronic, and Bundy has no final solution for them: Cuba; the high cost of defense; nuclear attack versus nuclear deterrent; deployment of defense forces.

On smaller problems, President Kennedy sometimes surprises his official household by working out the solution alone. When the matter of admitting Communist China to the United Nations came before the Assembly last autumn, the State Department was surprised to learn that the new little nation of Mauritania would vote yes. It didn't matter, because there were sufficient votes to keep China out of the U.N. In this case, however, the President wanted something done; he wanted Red China to get as few votes as possible.

At least twenty-seven persons, starting with Secretary of State Dean Rusk, spoke to the president of Mauritania about it. He happened to be on a visit to this country, and the diplomats used a velvet lever to try to pry him from his adamant position. He was a polite and friendly man, and he listened with patience to all the arguments. Each discussion was closed by the chief of state of Mauritania stating that his country would vote for admission.

President Kennedy decided to talk with him. The substance of what he had to say contained no diplomacy at all; it was more like man-to-man logic. "How can you say your country is neutral if you're going to take sides in vital struggles involving East and West? Either Mauritania is neutral or it isn't. It is impossible for you to be neutral favoring them or us. If Mauritania wants to remain free of influence from either side, why not abstain from voting?" That's what Mauritania did.

Diplomacy has as many keys as a piano. The sounds it induces are often dissonant, sometimes harmonious. President Eisenhower tried the direct approach, punching one key with one finger. He met with Khrushchev in sessions called summit conferences, and found too late that his confidence had been misplaced. In effect, the summit conferences took the business of the foreign ministers away from them and put it into the hands of presidents and premiers. The tragic weakness in this kind of diplomacy was that Dwight D. Eisenhower was an honorable man. He went to Paris, for example, determined to "talk turkey" with Premier Khrushchev, only to be shamed by the Russian demand that he apologize first for the U-2 overflights or go home. He went home.

The projected visit to Japan was another fiasco. Halfway to Japan, a nation which had invited him as an honored guest, Eisenhower was forced to turn back because of Communist student demonstrations. Mr. Kennedy has trained on the mistakes and the triumphs of his predecessors. He wants no summit meetings unless the fundamentals of an agreement are reached in advance by the State Department and the Foreign Office of the Soviet Union.

Almost all of his discussions with other chiefs of state have occurred in Washington. By Christmas, 1963, the President will have greeted a total of eighty-two. No other American president has approached that number. As a diplomat, Mr. Kennedy's weakness would appear to be that he concerns himself with everything and everybody. He tends to give his immediate time and attention even to matters which are not the direct concern of the United States.

In early November he cancelled an appearance in Chicago at a football game because of a revolt in South Vietnam. The revolt was not a small matter, but it was an internal one. The American military mission in Vietnam was in no danger, and the Navy had already ordered the Seventh Fleet to sail south out of the Straits of Formosa as a show of strength. If anything, the revolt enhanced the position of the United States in Vietnam. Still, the President was up and about in the wee hours, getting reports, assessing them, calling conferences, waiting in his office for General Clifton to arrive with the freshest bulletin.

He spends his energy as though it were limitless, and spends it indiscriminately. President Truman, on the other hand, accepted crises like the Korean War and the firing of a popular figure like General Douglas A. MacArthur with the philosophy of a man who is determined to do his best, and get to bed early. President Eisenhower administered the affairs of the nation from the remote position of a supreme commander, and sustained a heart attack. His confidence was in his immediate subordinates, and he paid heavily for it. After his illness, however, he seldom permitted more than three or four appointments per day, and except for the antagonism of the press, went through his second term with equanimity. The press could raise his blood pressure twenty points with one "misinterpreted" story.

At three twenty-five the quiet feet of George Thomas walk into the bedroom, and again he pulls back the drapes. "Mr. President, it is almost three-thirty." The President opens his eyes, blinks a little, and says: "Yes. Yes. Thank you, George." He picks up a phone to tell the White House operators that he is awake. The word is flashed up and down the offices.

Mrs. Kennedy awakens in her room. John, who has been prancing around his room, under a form of house arrest by Miss Shaw to keep him from disturbing his sister, is now permitted to race down the hall and across to his father's room. The little legs fly, the arms pump manfully at top speed. George Thomas, on his leisurely way out, smiles as he steps aside to avoid a collision.

The President barely has time to get to his feet to brace himself against the onrush of a low tackle. "Daddy, Daddy, Daddy!" the child says. "I'm going to play with Clipper and Charlie." The President crouches and says: "You be good to those dogs. They're your friends." John leaves without a reply, and heads for his mother's room. Caroline awakens slowly, and Miss Shaw helps her with a fresh frock and slip.

In ten minutes Mr. Kennedy has washed and dressed. He spends a few minutes with Mrs. Kennedy and Caroline, asking such questions as "What are your plans? Are you going out? I'll be in the office." At the elevator he is met by a Secret Service man and starts back to the executive wing. His manner is always one of self-assurance and graciousness, nodding to policemen as they stand at their posts—a man with an unremitting mission, a folder of papers tucked under his arm.

He enters the office through Mrs. Lincoln's door. The Secret Service man walks out into the hall and announces to the guards that the President is now in his office. Ken O'Donnell gets the news and joins the President as he studies a digest of the messages which have accrued since lunchtime. Some of these are from Cabinet members who pass knotty problems on to the President. This, of course, adds to Mr. Kennedy's volume of work, but he does not protest.

O'Donnell tells the President that Bundy and General Clifton are in his office. "Send them in," he says, and makes notations on some of the messages. The general, in slate-blue uniform, and Bundy, in a brown jacket, walk into the office, and the President leaves his desk to sit in the rocker between the beige sofas. He waves the men to be seated, because he feels that the ramifications of Mr. Khrushchev's morning speech may require time and discussion. Bundy tells him at once that everyone is agreed that the speech has no political value. This supports the President's original notion, and after a few moments, the visitors leave.

Salinger comes in and sits on the right side of the desk. He uses a few sheets of paper and a pencil to work out the matter of the press conference, and he goes over the probable questions which will come from the floor. In matters of national security, a president must be of two distinct minds: one which knows things which cannot be revealed, the other which must remember how much the public knows, and how much more it can be told without compromising security.

Some of the more delicate questions can be handled with wit, if one can summon the wit. The Kennedy Administration has been accused of managing news, and if this implies putting a good face on adverse events, and withholding certain news until the most good can be drawn from it, then the Administration is probably guilty.

In World War II, it was standard procedure for the Roosevelt Administration to denounce enemy communiqués as lies and half-truths. Certainly, that Administration felt no twinge of conscience when it minimized the damage in the Pearl Harbor attack, and it withheld news of the sinking of three heavy cruisers off Savo Island for several months until it could release news of a great victory simultaneously. Mr. Truman was less of a news manager than any of the others because he was blunt and cared little about press reaction. Mr. Eisenhower, through his press secretary, James Hagerty, could be snappish with the press when it asked too many questions, or presented calculated "leaks" of bad news for confirmation.

The President tells Salinger that he plans no lengthy statement at the press conference. The two go over the statements prepared to cover the most likely questions. These have been drawn up by the interested governmental departments to bring the President up to date on events of national and international interest.

Just prior to four o'clock Mrs. Kennedy, accompanied by the children and a Secret Service man, passes Mrs. Lincoln's office, looks in, and decides to stop for a chat. The children are fond of Mrs. Lincoln, and Mr. Kennedy's personal secretary seems to be happiest when they are disrupting her work, her desk, her neat folders, and throwing themselves on her in wild affection. She maintains one whole wall of her office for her personal collection of Kennedy family photos—mostly in color. Mrs. Lincoln has no children of her own, and despite her restrained and correct attitude, she has a deep affection for Caroline and John, whom she's known since they were born.

Mrs. Kennedy wears a pale lime sleeveless dress, and carries a matching jacket on her arm. She has flat black shoes on, no stockings. A comb is reversed in her hair so that it pushes the coiffure toward the front. She wears little make-up and no watch. Her only adornments are a plain gold wedding band and a tiny gold band on the pinky of the right hand. She sits for a moment, looking fresh and wholesome and attractive, and talks about the children. Mrs. Kennedy has evoked both admiration and envy by her ability to look smart at all times. A woman reporter said: "She could be in a barn, leaning on a pitchfork, blowing the hair out of her eyes, and she'd look like Miss America."

After a moment she is ready to leave. "I'm taking the children over to Mother's for a little while." She walks out to the car on the south drive, past the President's office, the Secret Service man a few paces behind. Caroline holds her mother's hand. She wears a pale yellow dress with a low waistline, sandal-type shoes, and a plain hair clip. John runs ahead, a microcosm of nuclear energy in a white sunsuit, a tucked-in blouse, and brown shoes. He wants to know where the dogs are. He would like to play with the dogs now. Smiling indulgently, Mrs. Kennedy asks the Secret Service man if the dogs can be loosed for a romp with the children.

The President has left his office. At three-fifty, still spending his minutes with care, he leaves by the southwest entrance, and with Pierre Salinger, heads for the press conference at the new State Department auditorium. En route, the two men go over the folder of reminder sheets once more.

They arrive under the ramp, where Mr. Rusk and Mr. Harriman are outside the lobby to greet the President. Policemen and Secret Service men have "sanitized" the area for an hour, and citizens and traffic are held at a distance. The President always bends forward to get out of a car, and comes up smiling, with hand extended.

The party goes inside to an anteroom, Number 3154, and a sheaf of last-minute bulletins is given to Mr. Kennedy. He sits by himself and digests them quickly. Across the room, a television set is tuned to an afternoon show. The eyes of the President dart from the sheets of paper to the set, and back again.

He calls Pierre Salinger over, and the two talk softly for a moment. Rusk comes over, a full moon of a man with the ready smile of the confident intellectual, and the three chat while watching television. They are still talking when the show fades out, the screen goes black, and the Seal of the United States comes on. At once, before the announcer can say that he now has the honor to present the President of the United States, Mr. Kennedy is on his feet, tucking his tie in, glancing over his shoulder at Pierre Salinger, and walking out of the room onstage in the auditorium.

The children are in the play area. Their mother sits on the edge of the canvas trampoline, watching and talking to Nancy Tuckerman and Pamela Turnure. She insists that they use the two-person bench. The dogs—several sizes, kinds, and dispositions—are chased by the children, who are, in turn, chased. The conversation between the ladies is not business; it is woman-talk—children, clothes, food, books. Caroline runs into the little playhouse and John runs after her. In a moment there is a yell with a note of alarm in it, and Mrs. Kennedy comes off the trampoline by reflex, until she sees both children emerge and run around the trampoline followed by the dogs.

"John," she says, "go down to the fountain and find the goldfish." The fountain is a large one, much farther down the lawn toward Executive Avenue; she is obviously trying to give the child something to do which will take him out of the area of running and falling—there are no goldfish in the fountain. John pauses a moment, and says: "My nose is runny."

His mother touches her finger under his nose. John runs off down the lawn, to the fountain. Caroline talks to the police dog, a black lean animal, and he cocks his head at her, ears up straight, and jerks his head from one side to the other, as though trying earnestly to absorb whatever wisdom she has to offer. He decides that what she truly wants is to play, so he finds a twig, snaps it up with his teeth, and offers it to the little girl. She decides that what he wants is to play, and she is prepared to indulge him. She throws the twig and the dog makes a big show of retrieving it and bringing it back to be thrown again.

John returns from the fountain, arms out, palms up, his expression a masterpiece of bewilderment. "No goldfish, Mums," he says. "Doggies chase all the goldfish away." Mrs. Kennedy squeezes his face with her hands. Her understanding of children is not confined to her own. A glance, a smile, and even strange children come to her side.

In Mrs. Kennedy's bedroom, Provey is at work. She cleans the place, including the bathroom, and sets everything to rights. Before the First Lady returns, Provey will have pressed some blouses and dresses and cleaned a few handbags too. The maid is alone, and she does her best work when there are no distractions. Others are at work too. Mr. O'Donnell is completing tomorrow's presidential calendar. Nancy Larson of the press office is digging out some close-up photos of the President from the file. These will be autographed within the next day or two and mailed out.

The policeman in the west sentry box phones the mansion to say that a caterer and his truck are in front. He has delicacies for tomorrow's state dinner. Mr. West's assistant gives the okay, and the truck moves in for delivery. Helen Ganss of the press office goes into the reception room to tell a California friend of Mr. Salinger's to please sit for a little while, Salinger will be back in about a half hour. Mr. Mitchell, the receptionist, takes the late-afternoon editions of the newspapers in to the President's office and places them on the table behind the desk.

Floyd Boring phones the chief of the Secret Service, James Rowley, on a routine matter and says that he has just received a call from Mrs.

Lincoln saying that the President would like to have an eye examination. Nothing serious, but he noticed that after lunch the newspaper type seemed to be blurring, and he expressed a preference for an ophthalmologist named Rones. Rowley tells Boring to send two men up to Dr. Rones' office now and to call in on the radio when the doctor is ready to see the President.

The sun is deep in the west. The men driving the leaf blowers on the White House lawn turn them off, and start to move the mounds of leaves into trucks. An usher switches on the big chandelier light on the White House portico; and an assistant in the White House kitchen begins to peel carrots. A messenger arrives from the Department of Defense with a folder for Mr. Bundy. It is taken, receipted, and placed on his desk.

Dave Powers has also been working on the President's schedule, and he is almost omniscient in knowing when one appointment is too close to another, or when two inconsequential ones are too far apart. The President likes to have them bunched tightly, so that there is little waiting time between. Often, when O'Donnell or Powers tells him that the next appointment is in the outer office ahead of time, Mr. Kennedy will drop his work and see the person at once. O'Donnell now goes over the list, checking the time allotment for each one and making a few minor corrections. He has been keeping the President on time for appointments for a long time. Ken's appearance in a room in which the President is chatting with guests is sufficient to move Mr. Kennedy into his farewell handshakes.

On the south lawn, Mrs. Kennedy asks a guard to take the dogs back to their room behind the flower room. The Misses Tuckerman and Turnure rise to take their leave. Mrs. Kennedy gathers the children together, finally ready to visit Mrs. Hugh D. Auchincloss, her mother. This is always a happy occasion, and it also helps keep Mrs. Kennedy in touch with her old Georgetown friends— friends who knew her before she met the freshman Congressman from Massachusetts.

Some afternoons she takes Caroline and John to a Georgetown bookshop, or to a Maryland farm where the three of them can lean on a fence and watch the horses at pasture. Others days she will drive to Glen Echo, or walk through Lafayette Park with them. Today, when she asks, "Now where are we going?" they say, "Grandmère's."

She gets in the front seat with the Secret Service driver and manages to squeeze the children in too. They all ride up front, threading the Washington traffic, watching the taxis whiz by, waiting for the lights. Sometimes Mrs. Kennedy drives, and then Caroline and John are all over the Secret Service man.

# 4:00 P.M.

Mrs. Kennedy arrives at her mother's in time to watch the press conference on TV. It always lasts a half hour or slightly less, never more. At the expiration of thirty minutes, it is pre-arranged that Merriman Smith will stand and say, "Thank you, Mr. President," and that closes the session. At the moment, the cameras are focused on a stout middle-aged reporter in the audience who is reading his question from a notebook. He wants to know if there is a "thaw" in the Cold War.

Mr. Kennedy grasps both sides of the lectern. Thaw, he says, is a relative word. To determine a thaw, one must know how cold it was earlier. He would say that Mr. Khrushchev's speech of this morning, in Moscow, sounds somewhat melting— this draws laughter—but it is difficult to anticipate whether this will be followed by warmer weather or the onset of another freeze. As he concludes each reply, the President looks over the tiered auditorium and sees hands raised. He studies the faces swiftly, and points to a hand. The reporter stands and announces his name. Then he asks his question.

Until last year, reporters were requested to announce their names and the names of their newspapers. This was abused by a woman reporter who represents a group of small newspapers. She saw the televised press conference as free advertising, and so she came to each press conference with waving hand, trying to be recognized. Each time she announced her name, she tacked on the name of a different newspaper. Salinger changed the rule, and reporters now give only their names.

There are twelve hundred persons who are accredited White House reporters. This too is an abuse of a privilege, because most of them are editors who never get to the White House or to a press conference, but who feel that the card is of some value to the holder. Of the twelve hundred, there are seldom more than four hundred at a press conference, and in the day-to-day coverage of the White House, there aren't more than thirty or forty regulars. These are the true opinion-molders, since they know the President and they know the premises and they can almost smell a burgeoning story in the atmosphere of the reception room.

Some like the President. Some do not. Some work for newspapers which, as a matter of policy, are opposed to Mr. Kennedy; others are employed by newspapers which support him. Some write their own stories each day and file them by teletype; some phone them in by direct wire. The regulars seldom ask witless questions like, "How long will the United States continue to support Nationalist China against Mao Tse-tung?" Or "Is it true that the C.I.A. is supporting the building of an anti-Castro invasion force in Nicaragua?" or "Is it true that you're going to pull our forces out of South Vietnam?"

As the President answers the questions, a government official offstage monitors the phone connection to the White House, so that if an urgent matter arises, the President can be reached at once. None of his predecessors had this sense of urgency. On the day Mr. Eisenhower had his heart attack, he was playing golf when he was told that Mr. Secretary Dulles wished to speak to him at once. It required time to drive the golf cart back over the fairways and across to the clubhouse. By the time he arrived, the ordinary phone connection had been broken, and Eisenhower had to make two more calls before he could speak to his Secretary of State.

When the last question is asked, and answered, Mr. Kennedy smiles and walks offstage. A few of the State Department officials and his own team flank him as he goes to the elevator to ride back down to his car. They tell him he did well. Sometimes they chuckle about a dangerous question which might have been asked, but wasn't. The President gets out of the elevator, nods to the

Secret Service men, and starts back for the White House, seven blocks away.

He comes in by way of the southwest gate, steps out of the car, and walks across the lawn to his office. The stride is swift, and he leads his guards as the head of a comet leads the flaking tail. When he sees familiar faces he nods and smiles. Like most presidents, he cultivates a prodigious memory for names, and uses first ones.

The latest messages are on his desk. He scans them quickly, tosses them aside, and glances at his watch. "Please send the ambassador in," he says, and O'Donnell escorts the newest diplomat. This is a short and formal ceremony, archaic and dull. The President expresses delight at meeting the new ambassador, and recites a short history of the long friendship of the two nations. The ambassador, usually in formal uniform, presents the best wishes of his chief of state, and also presents his credentials as ambassador. The President hopes that the new man will like Washington, and will remain a long time. Sometimes there are a few pleasantries thrown in. When Mr. Duke shakes hands with Mr. Kennedy, the ceremony is over and Mr. Duke escorts the foreign emissary out to his car.

Salinger is back in his office, ankles crossed on the edge of the desk, chubby frame in repose behind the cigar. "That," says Chris Camp, "was an unusual press conference." The press secretary comes out of his reverie. "How?" he says. Then he answers his question. "Oh, you mean no breakfast conference, and so forth. Well, that's the way the President wanted it today."

The President is a believer in newspapers as a means of world communication and he treats his press conferences as seriously as though they were diplomatic sessions. Normally he prepares for them like a college student who has spent too much time in the locker room and not enough in the study hall. On press conference days, Mr. Kennedy usually has breakfast with Pierre Salinger, Walter Heller, an economics advisor, Ted Sorensen, Dean Rusk, Lyndon Johnson, and McGeorge Bundy.

He brings a preliminary check list with him, and as they sit around the table in the main-floor dining room, he usually says: "These are the subjects on which I would like a little help." He ticks them off, one by one, while the men eat their breakfast, and each contributes what he can. Salinger makes notes. It is up to his group in the press office to find the correct answers to the questions.

Sometimes Salinger leaves the breakfast earlier than the others. He hurries to his office, and puts a staff of secretaries to work digging into the files and making phone calls to various governmental departments to get facts, figures, dates, names. At such times, the President often cuts short his afternoon nap and again calls in Salinger, Sorensen, and Bundy for a final rundown on press questions. Always he asks for specific numbers: How many tons of wheat? Whose ships? How much American traffic over the German autobahn? Which nations subscribed to that particular treaty? When? Did Senator Barry Goldwater vote for or against a particular bill? Did he make a comment? Is it in the *Congressional Record?* How much foreign aid to the Congo this year as compared with two years ago? What has that government done with the money? When?

"Come to think of it," Pierre Salinger says, "it was unusual. But, if you saw it on TV, you know he did all right."

# 5:00 P.M.

Mrs. Lincoln phones the Secret Service. Floyd Boring answers. "I was about to call you," he says. "Two of our men have gone to Dr. Rones' office. Everything is all right. They just called back by radio. Our men are waiting in the south driveway behind your office any time the President is ready." Mrs. Lincoln hangs up, walks around her desk, and peers into the oval office. Mr. Kennedy is alone. He is perusing the afternoon newspapers.

"Any time you wish," she says, "you may leave for the eye doctor. They're waiting outside." The President thanks her, and tells her to pass the word that he is out and will be back in about a half hour. The message is flashed all over the White House, from operators to office help, as Mr. Kennedy walks out onto the lawn. Two men fall in beside him. "It is probably nothing," the President says, "but it's good to check."

There are three cars. One precedes the President; one follows him. The drive is a short one, and as the cars cross Pennsylvania Avenue, the President sees the setting sun. He sees it with appreciation, and with regret too, because, to his way of thinking, day's end means that most of the four-hundred-odd persons who work in the White House are leaving for home. Mr. Kennedy feels that time is brief, and a man must accomplish many things. Sometimes the sun appears to zip across the vault of blue sky, here and gone in a trice. He is reconciled to the fact that no man achieves all that he sets for himself to do, but the President faults himself for not accomplishing more and ever more.

Two Washington Police Department officers stand outside the small building where Dr. Rones has his office. They keep the curious away. As the three cars pull to a stop, the Secret Service men get out, looking up and down the street and across to the far side; and they raise their heads to study rooftops. They nod, and a man in the car with the President opens the back door and Mr. Kennedy steps out.

A stout woman, studying some merchandise in a window, says loudly: "Oh, look! There's the President!" He disappears inside and goes upstairs. The doctor is ready. So is a nurse. It is possible that Dr. Rones had appointments with other patients at this hour, but he has canceled them for the President. A Secret Service man stands in the waiting room. He was the early bird, the man who examined the premises.

The doctor asks routine questions. The nurse checks the replies on a card. How long since your last eye examination? Have you ever had any trouble before? What is the trouble like now? Do you wear glasses regularly, or now and then? Read much? Ever get headaches when you read? Put your chin on this black object and look straight ahead at me. A little white light begins to pinpoint the iris of the right eye.

In the White House, Bernard West puts his jacket on. He gives the night orders to his assistant. The chief usher is ready to leave for home. Provey is on the third floor, donning her coat. She too is going home to her mother and her two boys. Nancy Tuckerman is stacking problem papers in a briefcase. Pamela Turnure completes a press release on the First Lady's work with the Fine Arts Committee on the refurbishing of the White House. George Thomas takes the elevator down, and carries a complete change of clothing for the President to wear after his evening swim. He hangs them in the dressing room off the pool.

In the east wing, Arthur Schlesinger gazes out toward the Treasury Department Building, across the street. He doesn't see it because his mind is elsewhere. Helen Ganss and two other women in the press office tidy their hair, then leave for home. The White House policemen at the several gates check out the regular personnel, and a sheet of paper before them tells at once who has been admitted today and how many have left. This is a balance sheet in people.

Dr. Rones finds nothing wrong with the President's sight. The eyes are healthy; the arterial structure is good; there is no pressure on the eyes from within; the vision is slightly less sharp than it once was. He finds a certain amount of fatigue, but this could be the result of exposure to strong sunlight while yachting or attending sports events, rather than from reading. The President thanks him, and leaves. A bill will be sent to the White House. The President feels relieved. He tells the Secret Service man in his car that everything is all right, and the cavalcade starts back.

At this moment Mrs. Kennedy and the children are going through the southwest gate, back onto the White House grounds. John's white suit is streaked with dirt. He had managed to fall into a pile of leaves. Mrs. Kennedy never permits herself more than a momentary vexation in matters of this kind. Sometimes she says, "Oh, Johnny," in a motherly wail, but between placid cleanliness and healthy childhood play, she is on the side of play.

On the second floor, Miss Shaw meets the family. There is a moment of conversation about the visit to Mrs. Auchincloss, and Mrs. Kennedy asks the children's nurse to put a fresh suit on John, anything that will last from now until bedtime. The children go off to their rooms. Mrs. Kennedy consults with the housekeeper, examines new linens and flatware, and then sits to examine the folder of papers, letters, reminders, and so forth, left by Miss Tuckerman for her attention.

About twice a week the President and Mrs. Kennedy have personal friends in to visit; sometimes for dinner and the evening. There are never more than two or three couples, and it is never formal. The schedule shows that no one is expected this evening. Two nights earlier they had friends stop by, and after dinner had a private showing of *Lawrence of Arabia* in the White House theatre.

There are dozens of television sets in rooms around the White House, but the President and Mrs. Kennedy seldom watch TV. Neither are the children addicted to it. On rainy afternoons, for example, Mrs. Kennedy often takes both children downstairs to the little theatre and has a projectionist put animated cartoons on. She sits and watches with them.

When the President gets back to his office, he phones Mrs. Kennedy to tell her about the eye doctor. He doesn't want the word to reach her through a secretary or clerk. He tells her that nothing untoward was found except a little eye fatigue. He will call later, when he is ready to leave the office for the swimming pool.

The Secret Service men park the cars and return to their posts. Their credo is that surprise is the best way of protecting the President from those who might want to kill him. A publicized schedule of any visit, any trip, any appointment presents a potential danger. The visit to Dr. Rones held little danger, since even the President knew nothing about it until an hour before the appointment.

Prior to the time that the work of guarding the President was assumed by the Secret Service, the White House guards were mostly Washington City policemen, men who were not dedicated to the work, nor trained for it: Lincoln, Garfield, and McKinley were assassinated. Even after the Secret Service took charge, there were several open attempts at assassination. An insane man named Zangara tried to shoot President-elect Franklin D. Roosevelt in Bayfront Park, Miami; two ultranationalist Puerto Ricans tried to kill President Truman.

There is always someone—usually deranged—who feels that he, and he alone, has been selected to rid his nation of a tyrant. He is a constant threat because he is unknown—a face in a crowd. Some of these people can relieve their feelings by writing unsigned threats to the President. Others do it by writing derogatory letters to their newspapers. But the quiet, persistent man, the man who, as Abraham Lincoln said on Good Friday, 1865, "is willing to trade his life for mine"—he is the most dangerous.

When it is announced that a president, on a

given day, will dedicate a statue, visit a hospital, review troops, visit a city, go to a football game or a concert, attend a rally, speak at a testimonial dinner—these are the times when Secret Service men examine the premises far ahead of time and co-ordinate their plans with the plans of the local and state police.

On his way to church, for instance, Dwight Eisenhower was a difficult man to protect because he always attended the same one—the National Presbyterian—and he always went at the same time. It was known; it was well publicized. So the Secret Service went through the church on Saturday nights from choir loft to cellar, examining everything including radiators and furnace. When the church had been "sanitized," they posted a guard and refused to permit anyone inside the church, including the minister.

Mr. Truman was the easiest to protect on Sunday mornings because no one, including himself, knew what church he would attend. He preferred a Baptist church, but his method was to walk briskly and aimlessly, going straight ahead as long as nothing impeded him, but when he saw a red light, rather than wait for it to turn green, Mr. Truman would make a right turn. Thus no one ever knew where the Sunday morning walk would take him, and no one knew where he might see a Baptist church along the route, and stop in. The assumption is that if a president doesn't know where he will be, then a would-be assassin cannot know.

President Kennedy is fairly easy to protect on Sunday mornings. He drives to Mass, as always with a Secret Service car in front and one behind. Sometimes he announces that he will go to St. Matthew's, but if he sees crowds in the street on arrival, he will change the order to St. Stephen's, or if he is in the mood, he will attend Mass at his old church, Holy Trinity in Georgetown; or at the little church in Middleburg, Virginia.

The Secret Service will work out a schedule of protection three weeks in advance if the President announces that he will attend a certain football game. Every bit of the route to be flown, and the airports, the routes of the cars, and the stadium itself will be examined and reported on. On the other hand, when he suddenly postpones a return to Washington from Hyannisport, as he did last autumn to attend a Harvard University game, the Secret Service men do not feel alarmed because his attendance is going to be a surprise to everyone.

White House Secret Service chief Jerry Behn has a framed bit of doggerel on his office wall:

Fame is fleeting, fitful flame
Which shines a while on John Jones' name
And then puts John right on the spot;
The flame shines on
But John does not.

# 6:00 P.M.

As the morning sun, many hours ago, painted the east face of the Washington Monument from the top down, so the setting sun now reverses the effect, painting the golden west side with gray shadow from the bottom up. The Lincoln Memorial is in shadow; the flag on top of the White House comes down; a bugler at Fort Myers blows the notes of retreat and listens to them echo out of the hills. In the Negro slums behind the Capitol, a woman sings "Summertime" in a tired, cracked tone.

Scores of thousands of girls are homeward bound, or already there. Home is a small apartment with two single beds and a daybed; home is curlers and chipped enamel and a pro-rata share of the phone bill; home is a place near the end of the bus line; home is anything but home.

Dusk lasts nine minutes in Washington. It dies in the light on the dome of the Capitol; men and women walk down Fourteenth looking for a new place in which to eat; the city glows like phosphorous to the captain of a jet at 31,000 feet; the lights are on in clothing stores closed for the night, they jiggle in front of a burlesque house, they look dim at the old Washington Hotel, they are brazen in a drugstore; in the old areas, the street lights shine through the leaves of trees, making them greener than by day.

This is the time when official Washington retires, and unofficial Washington begins to dress. This is the hour for snapping on bow ties while listening to the news on television; for locating snagged zippers on the backs of dresses; for giving the baby sitter a big smile; for permitting the children an extra fifteen minutes in exchange for the crime of going out. It is a change-over time—a time to prepare for a leisurely dinner; an evening of bridge; ballet at the National Theatre; a movie at Warner's.

Miss Shaw tells Caroline that dinner will be ready in about two minutes. The child is sitting on the floor in her room, trying to lift a doll's slip so that it doesn't hang below the hem of the dress. She says she will ready "in a minute." Her room is medium-size, done mainly in pink, with two youth beds with flowered canopies. Some of her toys are stacked in the fireplace against the far wall. There are dolls, stuffed animals, soldiers on horseback. She is on the floor because the love seat in her room is full of sitting dolls. There is also a giant giraffe and a large wooden rocking horse, and a canary cage. Each child has a canary. John calls his Bluebell. Caroline, who enjoys selecting names, calls hers Robin.

On the floor beside her is a small ironing board. Caroline is growing away from the giraffe and the cavalry soldiers toward real ponies. The ironing board and the dolls mean more than the little puzzles and games. She is neat and sensible and sometimes quietly serious, as though she comprehends more than a child of six should. The women who work around the White House smile when her name is mentioned. "She's a good, good child," they say. "She minds well."

A few minutes later Miss Shaw takes John by the hand. "Dinner," she says. He nods sagely and drags a little as he walks. Caroline gets up, leaves the doll on the floor, and joins them. The three walk down the hall to the small family dining room. Often Mrs. Kennedy joins them at the table although she waits to have dinner with her husband. John is put in a high chair, under which is a plastic square, and a plastic bib is tied across his chest. Caroline sits upright in her chair; sometimes with a cushion underneath.

Sometimes she corrects her baby brother. If he drops a piece of bread, Caroline exchanges a glance of feminine understanding with Miss Shaw. At other times his antics amuse her and, convulsed with laughter, Caroline becomes the little girl she is. When Mrs. Kennedy is speaking to someone and doesn't want to brook an interruption from the children, she extends an arm toward them in silence, palm out. Recently, when Caroline felt that little John was playing too rough, she adopted the same imperious gesture to stop him. Discipline in the Kennedy family takes the form of a speech of disapproval. A repeated offense may bring punishment by Mrs. Kennedy. But Caroline and John are normally good children, tractable, and not given to pettiness or selfishness. In fact, they live in a world of hundreds of adults, and will follow the suggestions and orders of all of them.

Most of the adults in the White House are indulgent toward them. This does not please their parents, who do not want the youngsters to feel "special" or "different" and who are happy that the children do not understand, in its broad semantic sense, what the word President means. Those who observe the President and First Lady with the children at first-hand—Provey, George Thomas, Miss Shaw—feel that the parents are succeeding remarkably well in keeping the children from being spoiled.

Affection from both parents comes without effort. There is nothing stagey or theatrical about the pleasure in their eyes when they see their babies. Mrs. Kennedy is a natural mother who can bring children up without apprehension, and without Doctor Spock. She does what her maternal heart tells her to do, and she can play with the children on the south lawn or race around a farm with them with complete enjoyment.

The President, no matter how solemn his mood, breaks into an automatic Kennedy grin when he sees either child. There is a little edge of baby talk in his attitude, and he often interrupts his work to crouch and talk to them on their level about their plans and play. He is conscious of the fact that both children will spend all of their formative years within the White House, and he and Mrs. Kennedy are determined to offset it by being full-time parents.

Many Americans were shocked when Mrs. Kennedy failed to show ecstasy at the thought of becoming First Lady of the Land. Some attributed it to snobbishness. Her feeling was that her husband's election would write finis to all her plans for a gracious and leisurely family life in Georgetown. Her fears were well founded. No matter how far she ran, the telescopic lenses were trained on her and on her babies. They caught her water skiing, shopping, sipping a drink, playing with the children, laughing with friends, on a yacht, on a beach, barefooted, attending a concert, sunning herself on a beach, smiling, frowning, talking, listening, lounging, in slacks, in bathing suit, in street dress, in formal attire.

After the second year Mrs. Kennedy learned to live with this situation and has found ways of keeping the children out of the world spotlight.

She will not co-operate, for instance, with reporters or photographers who try to cross the line from public life to private. It is possible, these days, to have friends in for an evening or have her father-in-law and mother-in-law as guests without creating news stories. Mrs. Kennedy is almost—not quite—beginning to enjoy her life.

Some First Ladies enjoyed the spotlight—Mrs. Roosevelt for example. Some abhorred it—Bess Truman comes to mind. Some took an uncertain position, half in, half out of public scrutiny—Mrs. Eisenhower and Grace Goodhue Coolidge. Some were completely retiring—Lou Henry Hoover and the first Mrs. Woodrow Wilson. Dolly Madison wanted to be a part of her husband's public life; Mrs. Lincoln was a hysteric who desired homage and obeisance and who countered an unconscious affront with unremitting venom. Mrs. Ulysses S. Grant would rather spend her time at her south Jersey farm than in the White House.

In the Kennedys, the United States has a young, attractive, and socially sophisticated couple. Americans who look for the simple, homely qualities will not find them here, because John Fitzgerald Kennedy and Jacqueline Bouvier Kennedy acquired the social graces before they reached the White House. They are readers of current books and magazines; they are students of history; they know which play is a hit on Broadway, and which one is a flop in London. They are at home in Paris or Rome, and enjoyed the use of a family plane before they saw a presidential jet.

Both are easy "laughers," gifted with a good sense of humor, and neither of them finds it difficult to drop off the plane of intellectual conversation to stories about children or anecdotes about themselves. At one time both Mr. and Mrs. Kennedy were newspaper reporters, and it is impossible to be successful in that craft without being gregarious. Mrs. Kennedy will not discuss politics, not only because her personal opinions might vary from those of her husband, but more important, she feels that he is a specialist in this subject.

In the President's office, the last of the mail has been signed. He begins the task of inscribing photos, and he does it so fast that one would have to know what it was to decipher the signature. Like other presidents, he has a stamp with his personal signature and, also like the others, he is not above permitting a secretary to sign his name to a picture. The requests for autographed pictures come in steadily, day after day, and if there is a point on which all presidents would find themselves in agreement, it is that this part of the job is drudgery. The work is barely completed when O'Donnell's door opens and McGeorge Bundy comes in with a folder of papers.

These are last-minute cables from abroad, teletype intercepts, mundane reports from nations which appear to have little significance unless viewed against the actions of other nations; military matters; common market reports, if they relate to something the President is trying to do; a proposal by the Strategic Air Command, routed through Mr. McNamara's office, for keeping more fully armed bombers in the air at all times; and perhaps a funny story about something which happened during the day.

Mr. Kennedy has again changed to a fresh suit and shirt. As the hour of seven approaches he asks Bundy to draw up a chair and sit down. Myer Feldman, a congressional legislative assistant, comes in with some bills to be signed. General Clifton comes in with a request from an American ambassador for a personal directive on a foreign matter, and leaves at once. Ted Sorensen comes in with a draft of a speech the President will make next week. He would rather have the President take it home with him than discuss it now.

The weight of office drops from the presidential shoulders. He gets up from his desk, stretches, and looks out the windows into the darkness. Salinger comes in with a late edition of a newspaper featuring the press conference. Among the many things Mr. Kennedy may say at such a conference, no one is ever sure what the newspapers will select to play up as the big story.

The men of the team talk about a variety of things. Ken O'Donnell comes in and sits on one of the couches near the fireplace. David Powers stands near the President's desk. The President leaves his office with the signed letters and photographs and puts them on Mrs. Lincoln's desk. He tells her to leave, that he has no more work today. She gives him a big folder to take back to the mansion tonight.

# 7:00 P.M.

Mr. Kennedy phones his wife. He asks her to ask the children if they would like to go for a swim with him before they go to bed. She knows they will. Sufficient time has elapsed between their dinner and the time their father will be ready for them in the pool gymnasium (seven-thirty) for them to digest their dinner.

In late summer, when Mrs. Kennedy was away on a trip to Greece, the President asked the children to swim with him in the evening. It turned out to be such lively sport, that he has continued the habit. They enjoy it, but their enjoyment cannot match his.

The President goes back into his office to the conversational wars. His desk phone rings and he answers it. It is the Secretary of State. The directive asked by a certain ambassador is already on Mr. Rusk's desk and he wants to double-check to make certain that these are the President's wishes. Yes, they are. They talk for a moment, and the President hangs up.

This is the "bang-board" hour. Anyone can voice an opinion; everyone is encouraged to do so.

The work is done, the assessment begins. Except for the White House policemen, and the Secret Service, the west wing is deserted. Only the machines in the Situation Room are manned, and these are watched at all times. When something big comes in, the watcher phones General Clifton at home, or McGeorge Bundy. Whether the President should be disturbed is solely within Mr. Bundy's discretion.

The President sits in his rocker. This time he does more listening than talking. He hungers for the candid opinions, because he must know whether the team agrees with his course of action. If it does not, he is prepared to defend his position and he expects the others to try to beat him down.

Pierre Salinger has a few requests from the press. They would like to have answers—or follow-ups—to current news. To some, the President will permit himself to be quoted. To others, the replies will be attributed to a "White House source." To a few, the President will make no reply because the story is in a state of delicate balance.

The conversation is always wide-ranging. A degree of joshing goes with it. Myer Feldman's reports of the doings on Capitol Hill are given serious consideration, because under the American Constitution, the Congress can rule by negation. It can not only deny the President the things he asks, but can give him that which he does not want. The elective body of representatives and senators, which in the second Eisenhower Administration began to split along conservative and liberal lines rather than the traditional Democratic and Republican camps, has drifted more and more into political coalitions of right and left. The result is that many Democratic votes which should normally be considered to be in the President's pocket are cast in opposition to his policies.

The group listens to a reading by Bundy of some telemetered intelligence from West Germany. It concerns the fiscal policies of the Erhard government, and as nothing in it runs counter to what the old Adenauer government had been doing, it is discussed quickly and dismissed. The men agree that the untangling of the European ball of yarn, after it has rolled through two World Wars in a half century, is complex. Germany, a defeated nation, is more powerful economically than Great Britain, a winner. France, a loser-winner, is not content to remain a second-rate power and wants to lead a third entity, unaligned with either East or West.

Some of the European nations are Januses—facing in two directions at once. Yugoslavia is one; Italy, which is Western in its sympathies, is Eastern in its voting. Spain, which is not admitted to NATO, gives four big bases to the U. S. Air Force. East Germany, with socialist ideology, lost its heavy machinery to the East, its refugees to the West, and its pride all over the world. A new regime in Nicaragua, an election in Sweden, a speech by Fidel Castro can start a lively debate. A loss of a gubernatorial seat, or the gain of a congressional seat, can start a four- or five-way analysis in which everyone gets into the act.

At seven-thirty the phone rings. The children are on their way down to the swimming pool. The President breaks up his conference with an order here and there, a glance at tomorrow's calendar, and quite often a reminder to O'Donnell that he wants to see a certain official sometime in the day, even though it is not on the formal calendar.

He says his good-nights to all, and they leave. The Secret Service man sitting outside the office is told that the President is on his way to the swimming pool. Mr. Kennedy beckons to Dave Powers, and the old friends walk out, having completed one more day of work, which, in two terms, will run to 2,720.

A messenger precedes them. He is on his way to the mansion with the President's night work. Mr. Kennedy's mood is as light as his step. The heavy cares, the imminence of grave decision are behind him for the moment. Now he will disport with his children, and he and Dave will talk of the light and amusing things: an Irish story or two, or the flavor of the Boston Irish which, at times, is a stronger mixture even than Wexford's.

The Secret Service man walks the hundred or so feet with them, and stands outside as they go in through a door near the flower room. The children are already inside; the happy—and loud— voices carom off the New England murals. The two men shut the door between, and undress quickly. "This," the President says, slipping into his trunks, "is the prime part of the day."

When the President walks in, the shouts of the two children approach a din and they run to grab his legs, to try to hug the heights they cannot reach. John is always full of grandiose plans. He wants to swim "all the way" up the pool with his father, even though he cannot swim. Mr. Kennedy slips into the pool, puts his arms out for John, and holds him in one arm while treading water. Caroline hangs onto the rim of the pool and kicks her feet to "make a splash."

Dave Powers swims close to her, watching that she does not lose her grip. The room is a bedlam of human sound—squeaky shouts and low-pitched voices; from outside, one might guess that a dozen people were in the water. At dinnertime little John had appeared to be tired. His inexhaustible generators had worn down. But now they appear to be restored, and he seems to draw more joy from being with his daddy than anyone else except Caroline.

John wants his father to swim underneath, "like a fish," and his father does it. Dave Powers can lie on his back and spout "like a whale." Caroline shouts, "Look what I can do," then plunges her head under the water and comes up dripping and smiling. John tries to do it, but he cannot force his face under the water, and he keeps shouting, "See what I can do"—and does nothing.

The phone at the head of the poolside buzzes, and the President swims to answer it, holding a finger against his lips for quiet. He has a whispered conversation, and everyone remains quiet until he finishes. He hangs up. Then he returns to the children and the bedlam of young shrieking is heard again. They cavort a few minutes more, and then the President orders the children out.

Caroline leaves, and goes into the dressing room to dry off. She is neat about this without being told to do it. Little John, on the other hand, will throw a white terry-cloth robe over his swim trunks and track the water all through the White House unless someone commands him to dry himself.

This time it is his father who lifts him atop the rubbing table, peels the little swim suit off, and gives the little boy a vigorous rubdown. John never stops talking through the entire operation. Dave offers to help, but the President waves him away. The two men talk about children, about home life as it used to be a generation ago in Boston, about John-John's prancing figure.

# 8:00 P.M.

The men part company outside the pool. The President says good night to Dave. They will see each other in the morning, when another, and more exciting, day will begin. The children, in sandals, run on ahead to the elevator and wait for Daddy. On the second floor, Mr. Kennedy says good night to the Secret Service man, then takes the children to their mother.

For a few moments the four are together with no intrusion. The President wears a fresh suit, and looks relaxed. He sees the fat folder of night work, and ignores it. Mrs. Kennedy talks about the visit to her mother's house, and of how John fell into a pile of leaves. At a time such as this Caroline curls up beside her mother, courting an arm to be put around her. John runs back and forth between the three persons who represent his life, and for a short while he seems to be working under a full head of steam again.

But the clock is a traitor. It brings the good things and it takes them away. Mrs. Kennedy says it is time for bed, and Miss Shaw stands near the door to the sitting room, watching. The youngsters stall a little, as children do, then they begin the round of good-night kisses and hugs. In a minute they are gone.

On the ground floor, Ted Sorensen packs his briefcase and puts the office lights out. As he leaves he nods good night to the guards at each turn of the hall, and walks out toward the west gate into the darkness. He passes James Rowley, who is sitting in a parked car inside the gate, just looking. The chill that was over the city early in the morning is back. It is not a cold night, but it is a night when a coat feels good.

In the press room, the night-watch reporters sit on desks, talking. There is no news for the night side, and they expect none. However, if something important should happen, these few men represent the news services and they can get a flash on the machines of newspapers all over the United States within three minutes.

An old-timer recalls the days when a newspaper could get a clear news beat and hold it for a while.

When President Warren Gamaliel Harding was dying in San Francisco, someone tipped the editor of the *Boston Transcript*. The *Transcript* made up a complete page one with black borders and a biography of Harding. This was before radio, and much before television, so that if the report turned out to be true, the news beat would be decisive. When the type was all set, and the page made up, a flash came in saying that the President of the United States had died suddenly. The editor dropped the news into a two-paragraph lead and told the printers to roll the heavy steel form onto the dumbwaiter. They did, but the dumbwaiter was not there. The whole page one fell four stories into the cellar of the building.

In the late hours, when there is no news, reporters tend to talk about other reporters, other days, other stories. Some play chess. Some play cards. The most difficult kind of reporting is to wait out the clock when nothing is happening. It is that kind of a night. Across from the press room, an officer sits reading a newspaper under a shaded lamp. A Negro usher in the reception room dozes in a leather chair.

Lights are still on in some of the offices, but the desks are bland and empty. In the President's office, a single lamp glows. Around it, a fretful housefly buzzes and sits. He can, if he chooses, sit in the chair of the President of the United States, but he is more impressed with the lamp. Outside, policemen patrol the perimeter of the grounds, walking their rounds, watching, hoping that nothing will happen.

In many parts of the city, the people who work in the White House are now at home. Each can be summoned by a White House operator at any moment. They seldom are. Some live in Maryland; others in Virginia. A few were born and raised in this city, but they are rarities. Most of these people are temporary dwellers. They come from Nebraska and New York and Utah and Georgia, and from Vermont and Alabama and California and Minnesota. They speak a common tongue with differing accents and idioms, and have common loyalties.

A waiter comes into the sitting room. The President and Mrs. Kennedy are in conversation and the waiter stands aside, waiting for silence. When it comes he asks if they would like a drink before dinner. Mrs. Kennedy thinks about it. "Maybe a daiquiri," she says. "Yes, a daiquiri." The President gives it a little thought. "See if you have a cold beer out there," he says. "A cold beer would go well right now." The waiter disappears. He knows that he has beer in the refrigerator off the small dining room because the President enjoys beer. Eisenhower was a Chivas Regal drinker; Truman liked bourbon; Roosevelt liked highballs. But President Kennedy is a beer man, and when he doesn't ask for that, he will usually request a daiquiri.

"My husband never brings his office into the house," Mrs. Kennedy has said, and this is true tonight. He will talk about anything except the nation's business. When Mrs. Kennedy wants to know what is going on, she consults a newspaper.

She asks if he plans another trip to the family home in Palm Beach and he says no.

Dinner is served. The couple continue their conversation for a moment, and then go to the dining room. The mahogany table is oval. There is a bright chandelier over it, and some scenes adorn the wallpaper. To the left is a screen, which covers the door leading to the kitchen. "What are we having?" the President asks. He holds his wife's chair out and she sits. "Lamb chops," she says. A soup, some broccoli with hollandaise, a baked potato, and a green salad complete the meal. There are blue drapes across the two big windows facing Pennsylvania Avenue and these are pulled back diagonally. On a sideboard are three silver hunt pieces presented to the White House by Andrew Jackson.

The table is set with President Monroe dinner plates—an eagle on a white base and a tile-colored rim. Sometimes, when the dinners are more formal, the Kennedys use the Eisenhower service, which has a white base with the seal of the United States surrounded by gold stars and a gold-figured rim.

The Kennedys used to spend some evenings visiting friends. As the first term draws to a close, the President spends less and less time out and more and more time at his work. "So much to do; so little time." He feels that his work requires most of his waking hours. He is also in the position of enjoying his work, so that the problems of "homework," which have worn many a president down to thin irritability, is as much a tonic for John F. Kennedy as a good round of golf.

His work and his hobby are one. He shows no signs of wear, even though some newspaper photographs, picturing him squinting against strong sunlight, are captioned as "indicating the strain of high office." The President's complaint is to the contrary—the 2,720 days granted by the American public is not sufficient for any man to achieve the goals he has set for himself and his country. And this, of course, envisions two terms of office.

He works at being President as though he had spent many years preparing for it. There is no procrastination, no hesitation. He makes his decisions quickly and precisely. His manner is always to weigh all the factors, make up his mind, and then point the way. The Bay of Pigs invasion of Cuba was planned before he assumed the presidency, and when it was drawn to his attention, he hesitated in the matter of how deeply the United States should commit itself in the internal affairs of a neighboring country. History may judge Mr. Kennedy to have been wrong in this, but right or wrong, he has learned that a president must act promptly. When in October, 1962, he warned the Russians to pull their intermediate-range missiles out of Cuba at once, he was going all the way, because if the Soviet had refused, the President had no alternative except war. He was right in that decision, and his adversary backed off. Still, he uses the power of his office judiciously, and plans his moves so that even when he is bucking another nation, he tries to leave that country a graceful way out without too much loss of prestige.

Today he brings all the problems—large, small, and potential—to his private quarters, but he will not discuss them with his family. He will sit in the corner of a sofa, legs crossed, working on these matters one sheet of paper at a time, while Mrs. Kennedy sits across the way working at her social homework. The President's workload could be lightened somewhat if he would permit subordinates to make more of the minor decisions, but he is a man who wants to be peering inside all of the federal departments at the same time, and he wants to have a "say" in everything that is done.

At dinner, Mrs. Kennedy acquaints the President with the plans for the formal reception tomorrow, the menu she has planned, the people who will be present. In this, too, Mrs. Kennedy is a rare person, because most First Ladies permitted the chief usher and the secretaries to work out the details of all formal functions.

The President sips a little wine with his dinner, and when it is over, Mrs. Kennedy asks if he would like to have an ice. He shakes his head no. He wants to get back to work. In fact, he is happy that there are no guests at all tonight. Some people believe that the President spends these rare evenings reading the mysteries of the British writer Ian Fleming. This is not so. Mr. Kennedy enjoyed reading Fleming's works on plane trips, when there were two hours of time to kill. At home both he and Mrs. Kennedy enjoy reading history—especially American history. Sometimes Mrs. Kennedy likes to curl up with a good novel, but it has to be a good one.

# 9:00 P.M.

In Room 324, George Thomas has ended his work for the day. He will read, or turn on his television set, or perhaps go out. He is a man to whom loneliness is not a hardship. He likes his room, and his privacy, and his freedom to be alone or to seek human company. He nods pleasantly to maids in the hall, but he cultivates few persons as friends. As Master Sergeant Moany was devoted to the person of General Eisenhower, so too is George Thomas devoted to President Kennedy. He has been with the President for a long time, and in the middle years of his life he finds that he has no other permanent interests.

When Mr. Kennedy's back hurts badly, Mr. Thomas will not retire early. He will remain up, so that he can help the President with the removal of his shoes and socks and trousers. But there is no reason for it tonight. George Thomas believes that the President's back never stops hurting completely, but he feels that unless the pain is acute, the man has learned to endure it.

After dinner Mr. and Mrs. Kennedy return to the hall sitting room. They relax and talk for a while. He asks about little John-John's cold. She says that his nose is running, but he has no temperature and she has not called the doctor. Mrs. Kennedy picks up her folder of work. The President picks his up.

The work is tedious, but not difficult. The First Lady is asked if she has any special guests she would like to invite to the welcome of a chief of state due in Washington in two months. Invitation lists must be ready now. She thinks it over for a moment, then says no. Sometimes a few personal friends will be asked to attend the reception and the diplomatic dinner which follows. At other times, the guest list remains largely in the hands of the State Department.

The President goes through his folder quickly. Bundy says that there is a nuisance fleet of Cuban rebels in the Grand Bahamas, and he is certain that they will make sporadic raids on the Cuban coast. What should be done *now* to dissociate the United States from these forays? The President lights a cigar and thinks this one out. In the evening, after dinner, he sometimes smokes one or two cigars—seldom more. The First Lady smokes cigarettes, but doesn't average as much as a package per day.

Mr. Kennedy writes his terse solution below Bundy's note. He asks Bundy to acquaint the State

Department with the matter also, and to ask them to refer it to the British. The President, throughout 1963, was in the unhappy position of promising not to assist Cuban rebels to overthrow the socialist government of Premier Castro, while, at the same time, hoping that the exiles could do it themselves with the assistance of the disillusioned people of Cuba. In fact, under the articles of the old Pan-American Union, all states promise not to interfere in the internal affairs of other Latin-American nations.

The big television set remains opaque and cold. This, too, as has been stated before, has been given up as a form of recreation. These days the only program which can make the President close his folder of homework and turn the set on is a Jack Benny show. He used to watch "Maverick," but he gave that up. Now it's Jack Benny, or a special coverage in depth of a subject, or nothing. Mrs. Kennedy still enjoys a good television play, but she has to be reminded to watch it.

They work now in silence, each engrossed in separate problems. Once in a while, the silence is broken by Mrs. Kennedy, who may ask the President for his wishes regarding a certain event, or a certain type of decoration. Other than that, they continue their labors while the others who work in the White House are out in restaurants, night clubs, or at shows or parties.

Still, the drudgery is ameliorated by its dual

nature. He has his work. She has hers. Both realize that it would be much more difficult if the President worked on his papers while Mrs. Kennedy sat watching him, with nothing to do.

Now Mrs. Kennedy gets up to walk through the double doors to the children's rooms. Miss Shaw is not yet in bed in her room between the two. The women talk in whispers, and peer into the gloom of both rooms. Caroline is sound asleep, her head half hanging off the bed. John-John is curled up in a crouch and he whistles a little as he breathes.

Mrs. Kennedy says good night to Miss Shaw, and returns to the living room. The time is early. It is five minutes to ten. The President has finished his cigar, and barely glances up from his papers as she comes back into the room. Her walk is vigorous, her carriage erect. She looks as bright as she did early this morning when the White House operators awakened her with a buzz on the phone.

# 10:00 P.M.

The conversation is now sporadic, not an entity with a focal point, but a series of disjointed thoughts. It is the kind of talk which occurs between husband and wife when, in the late hours, they begin to think aloud to each other. The President mentions that he received a phone call from Hyannisport. Mrs. Kennedy asks how everyone is. Everyone is fine. She says she's thinking of going to her bedroom to finish a watercolor. He thinks it is a good idea. But now she thinks it is too much trouble to get the pigments out and try to match them with the work already done. He suggests that she read. She says she would like to read, but she has too much work yet to do.

He smiles absent-mindedly at a paper he is examining. He says he feels the same way about his work; if you permit it to get a step ahead of you, it is almost impossible to catch up. Besides, he finds it difficult to relax if matters are still pending. They work on. She says she wishes they could go out for an evening or two a week to visit old friends; a little conversational dalliance over dinner would be good. It would be a good idea, he says, and they should do it soon. She knows they won't. The job of being President of the United States has, hour by hour, robbed him of time, until now his last symbol of independence from the work is to get to bed fairly early.

She does not reprove him. Some of the public life they lead chafes Mrs. Kennedy's sensibilities, but she does not complain because she knows it must be like this, and it would hurt her husband if he were to be caught between forces contending for his time. It required patience to reconcile herself to this demanding position, but she has made the adjustment and she smiles on the occasions when she plans an evening at home and Bundy phones, or Rusk, or General Clifton, and John F. Kennedy excuses himself and hurries to the International Situation Area away off on the ground floor, and remains there for hours.

As he completes each paper, each briefing, each problem, each report, he turns the paper over on a table beside the sofa, and, surreptitiously, she watches the pile diminish. Mrs. Kennedy does not, meanwhile, neglect her own work, not only the multitudinous tasks of running the mansion, but the letters, the telegrams which should be answered. Sometimes she makes a notation for a reply which, in the morning, Mary Gallagher will pick up and type. At others, she makes little penciled suggestions to Nancy Tuckerman regarding flower arrangements, or how to decline gracefully an invitation to be guest of honor at an august gathering in another city, or how to phrase the permission to use Mrs. Kennedy's name as honorary chairman of some charitable organization which does work for underprivileged children.

The President thinks he would like to have another glass of beer. Mrs. Kennedy puts her work on the arm of her chair and goes through the dining room into the kitchen and gets it for him. She pours it and puts it on the coffee table before him and suddenly remembers something funny that happened between Caroline and her "Grandmère." The President turns away from his work and sips the cold beer and listens. He tells her about the bedlam she missed in the swimming pool this evening.

She asks when his father and mother are coming to visit again. The President is back at his work. He says he doesn't know. Mrs. Kennedy says—impulsively—that she wishes his father lived with them at the White House. "You know how I feel about him," she says. It is more than admiration. Sometimes when his name is mentioned in a group, she beams the big open smile she has and says: "Just love him."

# 11:00 P.M.

The President looks at his watch. "I didn't know it was that late," he says. His wife doesn't hear him. She is busy examining another folder, and this one is a labor of love. It relates to the work being done by the First Lady and the Fine Arts Committee. It does not sound like much of a project, but it amounts to the most important work done on the decoration of the White House in this century. Most President's wives looked over the mansion, and figuratively threw up their hands. The many rooms were a hodgepodge of random art, faded furnishings, and glitter. For a hundred and fifty years Presidents and their wives had vented their whims on the White House, never refurbishing the whole—even in poor taste —but merely altering a wall or a room to suit themselves, without relating the alteration to the remainder of the décor.

The result is that the White House was one of the most badly decorated mansions in the world. The rooms were green or blue or red or white, and the paintings were hung willy-nilly, wherever a suitable space of wall could be found to hang them. The storage area was full of antique treasures—some rare and fine, some assorted bric-a-brac —but no one had either the time or the inclination to do anything about it. What Mrs. Kennedy did (and one might suspect she did it to give herself a full-time job and at the same time make an enduring contribution to the White House) was to appoint a Fine Arts Committee to survey each room and its present furnishings, take an inventory of everything in White House storage and catalogue the items, and begin the enormous task of decorating each room tastefully in the period it represents.

It is easy to dismiss the project as the work of a woman trying to put a "feminine touch" on the stiff austerity of the great public rooms. This is not so. Mrs. Kennedy and the Fine Arts Committee are, in effect, completing the great task begun by President Truman. He tore the inside out of the White House, restored it to strength as well as to its original character, and Mrs. Kennedy's work is to restore the décor, to augment, to enhance the elegance of the rooms.

Some of the paintings of presidents and their wives, which now hang in the public rooms and corridors, have been donated, since 1961, by private owners. One citizen found exactly the right material and the right color for two old Lincoln chairs. They now look exactly as they were when the Lincolns lived in the mansion. An American library room has been added to the ground floor. In it are thousands of books which relate to American history. It isn't a big room. A small antique table sits in the center of a rug and on it are hundred-year-old copies of *Harper's* magazines, neatly bound and lying open.

There is a room for chinaware. Breakfronts adorn the walls and dinner dishes are set against holders so that the dishes used by Madison and Jefferson and Buchanan and Taft are easily seen, and modestly labeled. In the center is a red plush ottoman with back rest, so that any visitor can sit in the center of the room and, by moving around the ottoman, study the pitchers and cups and saucers.

An ornate inkstand, made of bronze with a woman half reclining on the lid, is the only object in the mansion which was used by Thomas Jefferson. It was the gift of someone who heard about Mrs. Kennedy's project. The legend on it says: "T. Jefferson, 1804." It is in the Red Room. Ironically, the only wife of a president who cared to assume the burden of refurbishing a house which can never be a permanent home was Mrs. William Henry Harrison. She collected china from earlier administrations in March, 1841, and worked at it for one month when her husband died. As the widow of the president who served the shortest time—thirty days—the new president, John Tyler, permitted her to continue the work.

Mrs. Kennedy finishes her evening tasks. She notices that her husband too is nearing the end of the sheaf of papers he has been studying. To the outsider, the job of the First Lady, and the job of the President too, is a tedious, tense, never-ending task of trying to please everyone, everywhere, without ever appearing to regard the work as being tedious, tense and never-ending.

Mrs. Kennedy packs her work into a neat stack for the morning. There is still no sign of fatigue on her face, nor on the President's. He frowns, and sometimes smiles, as he reads the papers, but the Kennedys are still young enough to assume these arduous tasks without strain. She says she's going to bed. The President says he will be another minute or two.

The time is eleven thirty-five. Mrs. Kennedy goes to her bedroom. The President is now alone in the sitting room. In a Defense Department briefing paper he reads a newspaper columnist's critique which he regards as unjust, unwarranted, and untrue. He writes across the bottom of the page: "Well, any time they would like to take over this job, they can have it."

He sometimes uses this sentence around his office, but everyone knows it is an empty threat. Few men in the history of the Republic—with the exception of Richard Nixon and Thomas E.

Dewey—have labored longer and more candidly to become President. President Kennedy wanted this job and sincerely believes that he can do as well or better in it than any other aspirant. Mrs. Lincoln often says: "I just wish people knew how hard he works at being President." It is a reasonable assumption that Mr. Kennedy has no notion of giving up the job before the completion of his second term, and if he has the vigor and enthusiasm for it then as he has now, he will be reluctant to give it up then.

Conversely, he has learned to accept the jibes of the press without showing rancor. Although the presidential assistants often seethe openly at some of the attacks on the President, Mr. Kennedy exercises restraint. He has learned to cultivate a philosophy: "A man must learn to take it."

If he is slow to show rancor, he is equally slow to show elation. When the news is unexpectedly good, the staff in the west wing beams. But not the President. He considers the news as one word in a crossword puzzle. He will sit and mull it over and work out all of the other aspects related to the news (as though filling in the missing words) and then say, "It looks pretty good," which means he's highly satisfied; or, "It doesn't stand up in relation to the other components."

Mrs. Kennedy can become angry with friends, but seldom with strangers and never with servants. In a society addicted to the bland innocuous statement, she prefers to speak her mind, but she too has learned to be careful of words. When her husband was a senator, she could, in mixed company, hear a name mentioned and say: "Oh, I don't like that man." There were no repercussions in those days. Now when she is in a group, or in public, she adorns her face with a bright and friendly smile and always manages to say the right thing. The angriest her maid has seen Mrs. Kennedy in recent months was when Provey made a mistake in repleating a dress. Mrs. Kennedy's only reproval was to say, in a mild tone: "Oh, Provey, I don't like that. From now on, please do it this way." Mrs. Kennedy took the iron and showed her maid.

The President finishes his work. He puts the folder down on the couch, turns all the papers right side up, and sits for a moment in thought. He closes his eyes and rubs the lids with his fingers. This is the lonely time. While he worked, he had little time for conversation. Now that he has the time, the family is in bed. The strong face is half lighted, half shaded by the lamp at his side. The thick hair under the light is full of copper glints.

The policemen on duty throughout the White House are night men. The Secret Service men are night men. In the Situation Room the machines chatter, and there is a night man standing there to listen to their gibberish and to analyze its importance. Up in Room 324, George Thomas is still awake, and lies on his bed in a robe, reading. He will read until two A.M. and be up before seven.

The President stands and looks around the sitting room. He straightens his back and places the palm of his hand against it hard. Then he puts the lights out, all except one small one. If someone has to come in, in a hurry, and awaken him, the scattered furniture could be dangerous. The little light makes the sitting room look gloomy.

He walks inside, using his own bedroom door in case Mrs. Kennedy is already asleep. He undresses quietly and takes care of his nightly ablutions. Then he slips his feet into slippers and goes into the big bedroom. Beside his bed, he drops to his knees. The last few minutes of the day belong to God.

# POSTSCRIPT:

The foregoing was completed one week before President Kennedy was shot and killed in Dallas, Texas on November 22, 1963. Shortly after, while dwelling on the similarities of Presidents Lincoln and Kennedy, I wrote the following:

### THE DEADLY PARALLEL . . .

| ABRAHAM LINCOLN | JOHN F. KENNEDY |
|---|---|
| § He was in the fruitful middle years when the end came. Lincoln's heart's desire was to be known as the President who brought peace, at home as well as abroad. He did not live to achieve it. | § He was in the fruitful middle years when the end came. Kennedy's heart's desire was to be known as the President who brought peace, at home as well as abroad. He did not live to achieve it. |
| § He liked the South, but the South did not like him. Between the two stood the American Negro. The 16th President tried to force the South to liberalize its policies toward the Negro, but the South was neither ready nor willing to do it. | § He liked the South, but the South did not like him. Between the two stood the American Negro. The 35th President tried to force the South to liberalize its policies toward the Negro, but the South was neither ready nor willing to do it. |

| ABRAHAM LINCOLN | JOHN F. KENNEDY |
|---|---|
| § Mr. Lincoln had four children. Two were dead. In the company of little ones, he enjoyed shedding the weight and austerity of his high office. He enjoyed practical jokes, too. | § Mr. Kennedy had four children. Two were dead. In the company of little ones, he enjoyed shedding the weight and austerity of his high office. He enjoyed practical jokes, too. |
| § His First Lady was fashionable, but restive in the White House. She liked poetry, and painting, but not state dinners and the company of politicians. She fought to maintain a private family life, and sometimes lost. | § His First Lady was fashionable, but restive in the White House. She liked poetry, and painting, but not state dinners and the company of politicians. She fought to maintain a private family life, and sometimes lost. |
| § Mr. Lincoln enjoyed reading the Bible and could quote from the Old Testament as well as the New. His religious feelings were deep, but personal. | § Mr. Kennedy enjoyed reading the Bible and could quote from the Old Testament as well as the New. His religious feelings were deep, but personal. |
| § His program was often thwarted by his own party. Whatever support he had in The Congress came from a coalition of liberal groups. Mr. Lincoln had served in Congress after studying law and being admitted to the bar. | § His program was often thwarted by his own party. Whatever support he had in The Congress came from a coalition of liberal groups. Mr. Kennedy had served in Congress after graduating from Harvard University *cum laude*. |
| § In public, he displayed enormous patience, although in private he was irritated by the opposition to his policies in the American press. He was also beset by job-seekers and those who stole his time as though it were limitless. | § In public, he displayed enormous patience, although in private he was irritated by the opposition to his policies in the American press. He was also beset by job-seekers and those who stole his time as though it were limitless. |

| ABRAHAM LINCOLN | JOHN F. KENNEDY |
|---|---|
| § Mr. Lincoln was a spare eater who liked plain food. He was also an omnivorous reader who devoured newspapers and history books by the dozen. When he became President, in 1861, one of the persons most worried about his safety was John Kennedy, Superintendent of Police in New York. | § Mr. Kennedy was a spare eater who liked plain food. He was also an omnivorous reader who devoured newspapers and history books by the dozen. When he became President, in 1961, one of the persons most worried about his safety was Evelyn Lincoln, his personal secretary. |
| § Mr. Kennedy used to warn government agents to be extra watchful when the President traveled. Once, he sent detectives to Baltimore to make certain that the city would be safe for the President to enter. | § Mrs. Lincoln used to warn government agents whenever the President left his office, or whenever he made a decision to travel. She kept her office door ajar so that she could hear anyone enter or leave his office. |
| § Lincoln thought of assassination, but always fatalistically. "I know no one could do it and escape alive," he said. "But it is impossible to prevent it." | § Kennedy thought of assassination. Once, walking with Secret Service agents, he joked: "If anyone tries to get me," he whispered, "they're going to have to get you fellows first." |
| § When death came, it came on a Friday. The assassin was a misguided man with a gun. A bullet smashed through the back of the President's head. The killer was not supported by an organization. Mr. Lincoln was succeeded by a southerner named Johnson. . . . | § When death came, it came on a Friday. The assassin was a misguided man with a gun. A bullet smashed through the back of the President's head. The killer was not supported by an organization. Mr. Kennedy was succeeded by a southerner named Johnson.... |
| § After Lincoln's death, his son Robert lived at 3014 N St., Georgetown. | § After Kennedy's death, his son John lived at 3017 N St., Georgetown. |